Self-Hypnosis and Positive Affirmations: The Art of Self Therapy

Josephine Spire

D1392176

www.emeraldpublishing.co.uk

Emerald Publishing

© Josephine Spire 2015

British Cataloguing in Publication data. A catalogue record is available for this book from the British Library.

ISBN
978-1-84716-499-5

Printed in the United Kingdom by 4edge Ltd www.4edge.co.uk
Cover Design by Straightforward Graphics

ACKNOWLEDGEMENTS

This book is dedicated to my beloved parents Joseph and Elizabeth who are my inspiration, a big thank you to them for all the sacrifices they made to provide me with a great education, I love you tremendously and miss you everyday, thank you for watching over me and guiding me from up above, this book wouldn't be here without you.

I also express my gratitude to my amazing family for their endless love, support, patience, for holding my hand and standing beside me through thick and thin. I adore you all.

I thank all my friends I won't be able to name you all here but you know who you are, thank you for being there for me, supporting me and most of all loving me. I hope you know how much I love and appreciate your friendship.

A big thank you to Roger Sproston and your team at Emerald Publishers, it has been a privilege to work with you.

And last but not least I thank my children Alex and Ariana for loving me unconditionally, making me smile everyday and for enriching my life. I love you with all my heart.

·················

CONTENTS

·················

INTRODUCTION

There are so many things said about hypnosis but the most important of all is the fact that hypnosis heals! Hypnosis can be amazingly effective and is often directly responsible for major changes in people's lives. Research, studies and statistics indicate that hypnosis has gained popularity and acceptance as a part of evolution of our health care system and that a vast number of people are using hypnosis as a treatment or for relief of symptoms for both physical and psychological illnesses. Hypnotic techniques are safe and effective for quitting smoking, weight control, pain management, childbirth, anxiety, stress management, depression, insomnia, panic attacks, addictions, lack of confidence, nail biting, anger management, motivation, sports performance, treating and relieving phobias and also help with self-empowerment.

This book is designed for self-therapy which can be practiced safely with self-hypnosis, positive affirmations, relaxation and breathing techniques which all have a hypnotic component. These techniques should provide a basis for learning self-hypnosis for self-therapy. However you should always discuss your symptoms with your doctor first especially in cases of on going undiagnosed illness.

Positive affirming on the other hand is another technique for mind power, positive affirmations are very powerful that they give you the power to radically transform your life starting with positive thinking and eliminating negative thought patterns that stop you from achieving your desired goals. Its well known that what the mind focuses on it will manifest and that success or failure starts in the mind!

In my experience and thinking the combination of self-hypnosis and positive affirmations will yield tremendous benefit to your self-therapy process.

Why this book and how can it help you?
There are so many brilliant books out there about self-hypnosis and positive affirmations but there isn't a book that combines the two techniques. This book not only combines self-hypnosis

and positive affirmations, it also provides you with information, advice and further resources so that you can be fully informed about your condition and managing it. I hope that you find this book informative and helpful and that it will inspire you to make those positive changes that you need to make in your life by using the power of your mind and positive thinking.

Josephine Spire

....

Chapter One
A History of Hypnosis

Franz Anton Mesmer (1734-1815) is widely known as the modern father of hypnosis and the story of hypnosis follows on with one of Mesmer's disciples, who had originally been persuaded by his two brothers to join a new society called The Society of the Harmony. This was run by Mesmer himself with a little time on his hands on leave from the army. His first subject was deeply hypnotisable, falling asleep with his subconscious, however, staying awake, he could talk to the patient asking him questions and getting replies. He went on with others to find that his first patient was not unique after all. Mesmer discovered that the cures involved were not due to animal magnetism but suggestion. He went on to develop the eye fixation technique, the state that resulted from this was what he originally called hypnosis.

Dr John Elliotson was the first to demonstrate the use of hypnosis in British medicine. Before an audience of 200 medics he cured a dumb epileptic using Mesmerism and also used hypnosis in operations.

In France, Auguste Ambroise Leibeault and Hippolyte Bernheim (1837-1919) were the first to regard hypnosis as a normal phenomenon. They emphasized that expectation was the most important factor in the induction of hypnosis and that hypnosis works by mental influence. It is at this time when hypnosis was gaining acceptance and recognition that Sigmund Freud (1856-1939) an Austrian neurologist became interested in hypnosis and decided to visit Leibeault and Bernheim at their hypnosis clinic to learn their induction techniques, as he observed people enter hypnotic trances, he began to recognize the existence of the subconscious. The trance state is now widely recognized as a highly effective tool in behavioural change and healing.

Later on Milton Erikson (1901-1980) developed many ideas and techniques in hypnosis that were very different from what was commonly practiced. He believed that the unconscious or subconscious mind was always listening, he also maintained that going into a trance is an everyday occurrence, something that human beings do everyday for example when driving, listening to the radio, reading, walking, and other forms of activities that get the mind to concentrate and stay still. It is common and normal to go into a trance while you are immersed in an activity.

WHAT IS HYPNOSIS?

Hypnosis is a state of mind brought about by the use of a set of techniques. The word hypnosis comes from the Greek word for sleep. Hypnosis is a deeply relaxed state where your mind can help you to focus extremely well on any task that either you with self-hypnosis or your hypnotherapist suggest to help you.

Hypnosis enhances an individual's concentration and increases their responsiveness to suggestion in order to make the beneficial changes that an individual may wish to make in their thought patterns, their behaviours or their physiological state. Hypnosis used for therapeutic purposes becomes hypnotherapy.

THE MIND

The mind is an element of an individual that enables them to be aware of their surroundings and experience feelings, thoughts, actions and emotion. The mind can be broken down into two parts;

1- The conscious mind: is the analytical, critical and reasoning part of the mind that rules our awareness and understanding. It is the final processing point of our decisions, actions and reactions that we make in our lives.

2- The Subconscious or Unconscious mind: is the deeper part of the mind that is responsible for processing and storing a lot of things that we experience in our lives. It is also responsible for changes and reprogramming behaviours. When the conscious mind is switched off, the subconscious mind is awakened and this is where hypnosis suggestions, affirmations and visualizations take place. Unlike the conscious mind, the subconscious mind learns by repetition rather than logic.

LEVELS OF CONSCIOUSNESS

- Beta / Alert; is where the mind usually operates in daily life.
- Alpha/ daydreaming/ Light trance; is where the body is relaxed with slowed breathing and pulse rate.
- Theta/ Deep relaxation; here most of the conscious mind is switched off, the subconscious is at work with increased imagery. This is the state of mind when hypnosis is effective.
- Delta/ Extremely relaxed/ Sleep; the subconscious is fully operating in this state, dreaming takes place with suspension of voluntary exercise.

Hypnosis has been proven to be very effective in treating many conditions, illnesses as well as self-empowerment. Below are the many uses of hypnosis among others.

- ❖ Quit smoking
- ❖ Weight control
- ❖ Stress management
- ❖ Depression
- ❖ Anxiety
- ❖ Panic attacks
- ❖ Self esteem/Confidence
- ❖ Pain management
- ❖ Insomnia
- ❖ Childbirth
- ❖ Addictions
- ❖ Nail biting
- ❖ Sports performance
- ❖ Motivation
- ❖ Fear of water
- ❖ Fear of the dentist
- ❖ Fear of public speeches
- ❖ Fear of snakes
- ❖ Fear of the dark
- ❖ Fear of driving tests
- ❖ Fear of exams
- ❖ Fear of flying

- ❖ Fear of spiders
- ❖ Fear of water
- ❖ Fear of heights
- ❖ Fear of public/open places
- ❖ Fear of confined spaces
- ❖ Fear of death
- ❖ Anger management

More and more people are becoming aware of how effective hypnosis is, they are turning to it because conventional treatment isn't working for them. However, in hypnosis motivation is crucial, you must have the inner desire to make those necessary changes in your life. The ability to motivate yourself is very important, if motivation is coming from within yourself then your chances of achieving your goals are very high, on the other hand if your motivation is coming from someone else other than yourself, then your chances of success are reduced because you are not ready to change or you don't want to change.

Hypnosis and Suggestion
Suggestion is a useful tool in hypnosis and helps us to understand how the mind works. The power of suggestion is based on the psychological mechanism that whatever the subconscious accepts, it acts on. Suggestion should always be in the positive and repetitive. The whole idea to use the power of suggestion is to find a way to communicate to the subconscious.

·············

Chapter Two
Self-Hypnosis-What is Self-Hypnosis?

Self-hypnosis is a process where a person gives suggestions to themselves in order to gain access to the subconscious mind. Self-hypnosis is often used to modify behaviour, emotions, thought patterns, emotions and attitudes and for the process of self-hypnosis to begin you should be focused, totally relaxed both in body and mind. To gain access to the powerful tools of self-hypnosis, you need to learn how to induce a relaxed, trusting, receptive and open state of consciousness. Self-hypnosis can be used for about every kind of self-empowerment as well as reducing or eliminating physical and emotional distress. As a result many people have managed to free themselves of health problems and bad habits by learning self-hypnosis. Self-hypnosis is something that you can become very good at and learn more about with practice. Its important that you practice a few times each day. Hence repetition- visualization-imagery and use of positive language in present tense.

How does self-hypnosis work?

There are many benefits to be derived from practicing hypnosis on your own. Self-hypnosis can be applied to many areas of your life as you obtain the ability to talk to your subconscious. Self-hypnosis is a powerful mind tool to help you facilitate change through easy access to the subconscious mind. It easily enables messages to go through the mind and influence your thoughts and actions in a positive way. It's a quick and easy way to teach the mind how to relax so that new suggestions can be introduced thereby reducing, improving and overcoming many negative beliefs to create positive changes in your life.

Through self-hypnosis you reach a higher level of relaxation and heightened concentration and this aids new suggestions and new affirmations to be engrained into you. In other words you are more open to suggestions whilst all your senses remain fully alert and aware of what is going on around you throughout the whole self-hypnosis process. Before you embark on your self-hypnosis journey you:

- Think about what you want to achieve or change, and state your goal.
- Be realistic with the goals you want to achieve and what you want to get out of self-hypnosis, make sure your goals are achievable.
- Think about the time flame you want to achieve your goals
- What resources you will need to achieve your goal
- What you need to do everyday to be able to stay on the right course towards achieving your goal
- What problems you need to tackle to achieve your goal
- How you want to be feeling and thinking after you have reached your goal
- What you will need to do to make sure that you maintain your goal once you have achieved it.

Breathing exercise:

Correct breathing is a very important tool in self-hypnosis as it is in everyday health. When you go into self-hypnosis you will notice that breathing in and out deeply will help you go into a trance, enable you to stay alert and also relax you:

- Find a quiet and comfortable place
- Any position that is comfortable for you will do as long as you make sure your back is straight.
- Start breathing in relaxing your stomach at the same time as though it's filling with air
- After filling your stomach with air, keep breathing in and feel your rib cage expand
- Hold your breath for a moment then begin to breath out slowly
- As you breath out slowly, relax your chest and rib cage while you pull your stomach in to let the remaining air out.
- Close your eyes and concentrate on your breathing
- Relax all your body and mind
- Feel completely relaxed

Relaxation technique

Close your eyes and sit back comfortably with your feet together .... hands resting on the sides of the chair or on your thighs .... take a nice deep breath and begin to relax .....breath in again and hold your breath ...... then let go of it and feel yourself letting go of all the stress and tension as you breath out ...... just think about relaxing every muscle in your body from your head to your toes ...... and keep breathing deeply in and out ...... feeling the calm and relaxation flowing through your body relaxing you all over .... every time you breath out you become more and more completely relaxed ...... now think about nothing else but how your body feels ..... continuing to breath in and out ...... now focus on the muscles around your eyes and around your mouth ...... let them relax ...... and the muscles in your jaw are completely relaxed too .....feel them relax even more as you drift and float into a deeper level of relaxation ...... let the muscles in your neck and shoulders relax ...... feeling you with soothing relaxation .... the relaxation spreads to muscles in your back ...... running down your arms and your finger tips as you continue to breath in and out feeling completely relaxed .... now I want you to notice this same feeling moving to your chest, stomach and thighs ...... you breath in and relax these muscles and as you breath out you relax the muscles in your legs .... to the tips of your toes .... your whole body is covered with a complete sense of relaxation ..... you are floating deeper .... and deeper ....now count from one to five and as you count from one to five ...... you will let yourself sink more and more deeply into this nice relaxed state ...... One ..... deeper and deeper ...... Two ...... you feel more and more relaxed ..... Three ..... you are sinking deeper and deeper ...... Four ...... you feel so heavy and relaxed ..... Five ...... Now that you're so deeply relaxed ...... imagine yourself in your special place ...... a place that means a lot to you and makes you feel loved, happy, calm and at peace ...... feel it and imagine it ...... enjoy these tranquil feelings and keep them with you ...... allow these feelings to grow stronger and stronger and spread through all your body and mind ..... you feel good inside and out in this place

...... with a sense of tremendous well being surrounding you ...... and these positive feelings will remain with you for a long time ......

You can remain in this relaxed state as long as you wish ...... when you're ready count from one to five ...... slowly feeling your body returning to its normal state ...... and your mind becoming more alert ...... on a count of five you will open your eyes and you will feel relaxed, calm and wonderful ......

The benefits of a relaxation technique are;

- It slows the heart rate
- Lowers blood pressure levels
- Slows down the breathing rate
- Reduces activity of stress hormones
- Increases blood flow to major muscles
- Reduces muscle tension
- Improves mood
- Reduces anger
- It boosts confidence

How to use self-hypnosis

- Read your script several times before you record it so that you can become used to it and comfortable with it.
- Find a place that is quiet with no disturbance or background noises, record your script in your normal voice at a relaxed pace, slowing down and softening your voice which helps you to enter hypnosis. You can ask someone to record it for you if you prefer, whatever works for you, there is no right or wrong, whatever feels comfortable for you.
- The tone of voice should be calm, confident, relaxed, caring, soothing. As you leave hypnosis your voice can return to normal. Beware of background noises such as television, radio, and other noises that will interfere with the hypnosis.
- Do not forget to add a special place into the script if you want it in , this has to be a unique place for you where you can be alone, a place filled with peace and positivity, it can be a place you have visited or an imaginary one, a childhood cherished home with happy memories, a

15

beach, lake side, the woods, the mountains, a beautiful garden, by the river, in a log cabin by the fire, the savannah woodlands filled with wildlife, or any other place that you love, feel happy, loved, safe and secure there.

- After recording your script choose a place where you can be completely comfortable and relaxed with no interference, switch your phone, radio, television off and any other background noise. If you choose to sit on chair make sure that your legs are uncrossed, if you choose to lie down on a couch or bed be aware of not falling asleep half way through the self-hypnosis!

- Breath in and out and let your body relax, you can leave your eyes open or close them, breath in and out with each breath feeling your body relax more and more and take your time to feel all the stress and tension leave your body relaxing more and more.

- Start your recorded self-hypnosis script and after your session give yourself time to relax and enjoy the calming effect of hypnosis.

- Try and set a time aside every day for practicing, twice a day at least. Don't forget success comes from perseverance.

Why self-hypnosis?

Self-hypnosis is empowering and it helps you develop a self-help plan that keeps you in charge and in control of your life. The skills you learn will help you in various aspects of your life. It is also very fulfilling to know that you can address problems on your own and not rely on other people. It promotes self-worth and boosts confidence.

- With self-hypnosis you can re-design and change your script to whatever suits you at any given time based on your choice, needs and what works for you.

- You save a great deal of money and time with self-hypnosis as it's well known that going to a therapist for hypnotherapy sessions is very expensive so by adapting self-hypnosis you are not only saving money but also saving time to and back from sessions.

- Self-hypnosis is also private which can save you the embarrassment of sharing private Issues that you don't feel comfortable sharing with others.

........·.......

16

Chapter Three
Positive Affirmations-What Are Affirmations?

Affirmation is the act of affirming or confirming that something is true. Positive affirmations can help develop a powerful positive attitude to life in most areas of our lives for instance work, finances, family, relationships and health. Affirmations work because your subconscious mind accepts whatever you say to it. Affirming positively is a very powerful way to make those changes and achieve your dreams. The power of our thoughts is limitless and incredible, as our thoughts affect how we feel and act, if you feel positive you act in a positive way and on the other side if you feel negative your actions and behaviour will reflect that. When you have a belief in yourself that you are a success your mind is going to work towards nothing but success, because you are feeling it and if you think about being a failure you are going to feel it and your thoughts and mind will manifest failure. The thoughts that pass through our minds are responsible for everything that happens in our lives because as human beings we act on our thoughts.

Working with affirmations is a great way to create change as affirmations are very effective when used properly and consistently. As well as helping to make changes affirmations are also a great way for removing negative thoughts.

Continually repeating affirmations with passion will eventually breakdown even the strongest resistance. Once the resistance is broken, the subconscious mind will re- programme your old beliefs and learned habits thereby changing the way you think, feel and act because you have replaced the old negative patterns with new positive ones and then the changes in your life will start to take place. Any success has to be achieved in the mind first and then the body will follow.

How affirmations work

Affirmations work because they have the ability to programme your mind into believing whatever you are affirming and this happens for the reason that the mind doesn't know what is real and what isn't. For instance if say you are happy over and over again you will find that you will start to feel happy feelings flowing through you and even smiling and if you state that you are sad, that's exactly what you are going to feel, very sad. To write your own affirmations;

- Make a list of the things that you always think negatively about, it might be you feel judged by others and you feel unworthy, you are critical of yourself, ashamed of your choices in life, your habits, the way you look, it can be anything negative.

- Now write out affirmations but rather than saying "I am an unworthy person" say " I am worthy and deserve all the good things in life" then repeat your affirmations to yourself or you can ask someone to do it for you. Affirming at least five or more times a day will help reinforce the new beliefs.

- Affirmations work better when you are in a relaxed state of mind, when the subconscious mind is more open to the suggestions you are giving it.

How to use affirmations

- Affirmations should be used in the present tense or in the now.
- They have to be repeated three to five times or more a day, every day, until you achieve your goal. You can say them out loud or mentally whatever suits you whenever you can. Remember to be persistent and patient.
- Have passion and feeling when you are affirming and try not to think of negative things, maintaining the positivity is crucial.
- You can record your affirmations and listen to them when you're relaxed in a quiet and comfortable room.

....

Chapter Four
Quit Smoking

Many studies have shown that hypnosis is the single most effective way to quit smoking with long term results. Smoking can be an addiction or a habit. Cigarettes contain the drug nicotine which creates addiction that makes a smoker want to smoke again and again thereby reinforcing the addiction. Nicotine is an addictive drug that makes you physically and psychologically dependent on it. This means that when you stop smoking you get nicotine withdrawal symptoms. It's what nicotine does in the brain that makes it responsible for the highs people get from smoking and the negative feelings when smokers try to quit.

It is estimated that there are around 4000 different chemicals in the ignited smoke of cigarette and below are the most common ones;

What is in a smoke?

Nicotine; this is a poison and the substance that causes cravings as it builds up in the body and remains overnight. It is a well known poison causing nausea, vomiting pain, confusion, low blood pressure, coma and death. People die from nicotine poisoning usually from swallowing pesticides that contain it. It also contributes to heart disease.

Carbon-monoxide; is an invisible odourless gas that starves the body of oxygen causing cardiovascular disease. When inhaled, it combines with the blood, preventing the efficient absorption of oxygen. It contributes to low birth weight in babies of women who smoke in pregnancy.

Tar; is a sticky black residue containing hundreds of chemicals, some of which are classed as hazardous waste.

Hydrogen cyanide, ammonia, nitrogen dioxide; all these chemicals paralyse the tiny-hair like brushes knows as cilia in the respiratory system, making the lungs more sensitive to cancer causing chemicals because the cilia are responsible for clearing the lungs of dust and mucus.

Naphthylamine and Nitrosamines; these chemicals cause lung cancer and when absorbed into the body they contribute to other cancers.

Why people smoke

People smoke for a number of reasons and some of them are listed below;

- Addiction
- Smoking helps them relax and feel good when they are stressed
- Peer pressure mostly common in teenagers, they smoke because they want to fit in, fear being labelled boring and wanting to look cool.
- As a way of socialising
- Smoking as a way to pass time
- To lose weight or weight control- smoking reduces the a person's sense of taste and smell thereby reducing their appetite.
- Experimenting and curiosity

Smoke related illnesses

There are many forms of cancers caused by smoking that you should be aware of:

- Lung cancer- This is at the top of the cancer death chart. Amongst the symptoms are persistent coughs, hoarseness, pneumonia or bronchitis.
- Bladder cancer- It is estimated that about half of bladder cancer death can be related to smoking.
- Oesophageal cancer- This type of cancer is on the increase and due to the fact that the condition is usually advanced before diagnosis can be made, there is only about a 10% five year survival rate.
- Oral cancer- Smoking cigars, cigarettes or pipes increases the risk of this cancer by 60% and treatment can involve the removal of the larynx. Also the incidence and death rate due to cancer of the stomach, kidney, pancreas, leukaemia are also linked to smoking.
- Cardiovascular disease- is the main cause of death due to smoking.

20

- Chronic Obstructive Pulmonary Disease (COPD) a number of conditions that block the airflow out of the lungs and make breathing very difficult.-
- Emphysema-is breathlessness caused by damage to the microscopic air sacs in the lungs.
- Chronic bronchitis – the inflammation and narrowing of the airway tubes causing coughs with a lot of mucus.
- Smoking increases blood pressure causing hypertension, stroke and heart attacks.
- It causes fertility problems in both men and women
- Worsens asthma
- It damages the blood vessels the eyes and also causes macular degeneration
- Smoking causes periodontitis a dental disease that affects the gum and bones that support the teeth.
- It also causes low bone density in older women and hip fractures in both men and women.

Benefits of giving up smoking

Reduces risk of smoke related illnesses and death hence living longer Stopping smoking saves money as it is a very expensive habit

- Better sex - smoking improves the body's blood flow therefore improving sensitivity.
- Good dental hygiene
- Improves smell and taste
- Less stress which is caused by withdrawal symptoms
- Improves fertility in both men and women and the chances of giving birth to a health baby
- Improves eye health
- Healthy skin
- Fresh smell- breath, home, clothes, hair, car
- Non-smoking sets a good example to children
- It Improves self-confidence by making you feel in control

When you stop smoking

In 20 minutes - blood pressure and heart rate return to normal.

In 8 hours - nicotine and carbon monoxide start to leave your body and oxygen levels return to normal.

In 24 hours - your lungs start to clear out mucus and other smoking toxins

In 48 hours - nicotine has been eliminated from your body and your sense of smell and taste both improve.

In 2- 12 weeks – Exercise becomes easier and your breathing improves.

In 3-9 months – Any coughs, wheezing and breathing problems are reduced as the lungs repair.

In 1 year – Your risk of coronary heart disease is now half that of a smoker.

Remember that belief is very important in the stop smoking process, previous studies show that people who believe that they can quit smoking have a higher chance of succeeding.

Together with self-hypnosis and positive affirmations part of having an efficient stop smoking plan is to keep a diary for a week and record your smoking habit, this will get you to understand the reasons why you smoke. In your diary you record;

- Where you smoke
- The time you smoke
- The company you keep when smoking
- What you are doing when you're smoking
- How you are feeling when smoking
- And how you feel after smoking
-

QUIT SMOKING SCRIPT

I will take a nice deep breath and close my eyes .... I will begin to relax .... slowly going in a deeper state of relaxation .... I will take another deep breath in and hold it ...... then let it go .... relaxing ...... relaxing .... relaxing ...... my mind is relaxing more and more as I go deeper and deeper into a state of deep relaxation .... feeling all the tension leave my body as I continue to breath in and out ...... feeling calm as the relaxation flows through my mind and body each time I breath out ...... each and every muscle in my body is beginning to relax....... everything is peaceful and quiet ....

- One, the muscles in my face are relaxing, relaxing, relaxing ......

-Two, the muscles of my neck are slowly loosening and are relaxing, relaxing, relaxing ......

-Three, the muscles of my shoulders are loosening their stiffness and are relaxing, relaxing ....

-Four, both my hands are totally free and their muscles are relaxing, relaxing, relaxing ....

-Five, the muscles in my stomach are relaxing and loosening up, I am floating deeper and deeper into a soothing relaxation ....

And now I am feeling the muscles in my legs and toes relax, my entire body feels very comfortable ...... just drifting and floating ...... deeper, deeper relaxed ......

As I am relaxing deeper and deeper ...... I begin to imagine a very peaceful and very special place for me ..... I can see it ...... and feel it ...... I am alone and there is no one to disturb me ..... I can feel a sense of positive feelings in this peaceful place ...... growing stronger and stronger .... and relaxing me deeper and deeper....... I can feel all the stress leaving my body .... and all tension bouncing off and away from me ...... bouncing away ....from me.

And these positive feelings will stay with me and grow stronger and stronger throughout the day ..... tomorrow and the days after ......

Now that I'm in my special place and deeply relaxed I reflect for a moment on all the things I have achieved in the past ...... the goals I have reached and all of the positive things in my life ...... I feel proud of myself and have no doubt that I will continue to achieve more goals in every area of my life ..... I'm more determined than ever before to reject my habit of smoking cigarettes ...... I have all the right reasons to be a non-smoker ...... for my health ....my family ..... and my finances ..... my body and mind rejects smoking

..... I Imagine myself throwing a packet of cigarettes out of the window away from me and that feels fine ....

I reject my smoking habit ...... my lungs no longer want those poisonous fumes in them ..... they will now become clean .... clear and healthy once again ...... the smell of cigarettes is now disgusting ...... and the taste is unappealing and unappetising ......my mouth is clear of smoke .... without any trace of cigarette taste and it feels fresh ...... my taste buds experience the appetising fresh tastes of food ...... and that feels wonderful ....

There are no poisonous fumes in my system any more ...... I choose to be healthy ...... to breath clean air ...... my lungs are clean and healthy ...... I'm a non-smoker and have made up my mind ...... and I am now more motivated than ever to continue creating the most healthy and positive life for myself ...... and I am now a non-smoker ...... I feel it within .... I now make a conscious choice not to smoke ...... and emotionally I feel fine..... I'm a non- smoker and will remain a non- smoker ...... I see myself doing my daily routines without a cigarette ..... and feeling fine ..... being a non-smoker suits me just fine. I have now new ways of dealing with my old habits ..... when I'm at work I will go for a walk at break time rather than smoking ..... or I will make a cup of tea ..... eat an apple ....or join my non-smoking work mates ..... and at social events I will join the non-smokers ...... or go out with non-smoking friends ..... and at home I will read a book I like ...... go for a walk ...... or make a cup of tea ...... these are my new ways of dealing with my old smoking habit ...... it is a successful way ..... it works and I feel fine .... every day as I give up smoking I can feel more and physically and mentally strong and fit ...... and my outlook on life is much happier and healthier .... I imagine my daily routine without a cigarette ..... calm and relaxed ..... and there is a smile on my face ...... and I feel just fine .... it feels wonderful ..... if I'm offered a cigarette I will refuse politely as I'm stronger now ...... and I will remind myself that smoking is poisonous for my body and mind ...... and because I'm a non-smoker I begin to notice that every aspect of my life begins to improve more and more ...... every day and night ...... I breath more easily and have new found energy ...... I am a non-smoker ..... I enjoy being a non-smoker ...... and with my new ways of coping I am in total charge ...... I enjoy the benefits of being a non-smoker...... It feels great without a cigarette .... and I am proud of myself and my achievement .... of stopping smoking ...... I AM A NON SMOKER ......

I will continue to enjoy my special place for a few more minutes .... enjoying the positive feelings and relaxing .... floating higher and higher into a deep relaxation .... and when I'm ready to come back to full awareness I will count from one to five ...... and as I count from one to five .... my mind will return to its normal alertness .... and on the count of five my eyes will be open ...... and I will come back feeling .... calm .... peaceful ...... and relaxed .....

1. .... Beginning to come back ....

2 .... Coming up

3 .... Feeling relaxed

4 .... Beginning to open my eyes

5 .... I open my eyes and come back feeling wonderful

QUIT SMOKING AFFIRMATIONS

Affirmations to quit smoking are what is missing in most stop smoking programmes. Together with quit smoking self-hypnosis I believe you will get most success using more than one method at a time.

- I am now and forever smoke free.
- I cancel smoking out of my life
- I prefer life over death
- I refuse to give in to smoking
- I am smoke free and craving free from nicotine
- I successfully quit smoking and I'm more healthier, less stressed and happy
- I love myself more than I love smoking.

- I say yes to life and no to smoking.
- I love fresh air and detest smoking.
- I am a calm and relaxed non-smoker.
- I choose to breathe fresh air into my lungs.
- I am in control of my cravings and I only crave those things that are healthy for me.
- My breath, my clothes, my home and my hands smell fresh and clean all the time.
- I am living a long and healthy life free of smoking
- My body is becoming healthier as I continue to be smoke free.
- I look and feel great.
- My breathing is improving each and every day.
- I enjoy eating because my food tastes better than it has ever before
- My body is clean and pure.
- The energy of health flows freely throughout my body.
- I am in control of my life.
- I choose only to put healthy food in my body.
- I choose good health.
- As a non-smoker my body is free to return to perfect health.
- I enjoy living a healthy life smoke free.
- I release any need to smoke and accept a healthy smoke free life with open arms.
- Smoking has no place in my life anymore
- From now I will live a smoke-free life
- I am healthier as a non-smoker than ever before
- I am a non-smoker.

···················

Chapter 5
Weight Loss

Weight loss is a decrease in body weight and obesity is defined as carrying too much body fat for your height and gender, to the extent that it poses a risk to health. Losing weight has to be done the healthy way and can't happen over night with a quick fix. It requires long term commitment and changes in your lifestyle. For successful weight loss, time, motivation, dedication and effort together with a vast amount of physical and mental strength are required to make lasting positive changes with realistic goals. A person will be considered medically obese if their body mass index (BMI) is 30 or greater, an ideal BMI will be between 20 and 25: BMI is worked out by ;

1. Squaring a person's height in metres

2. Dividing the result by their weight in kilograms.

   For example if a person was 1.75 metres tall and weighed 70 kg then their BMI will be calculated as follows;

   1.75x1.75= 3.06

   70/3.06= 22.88

   22.88 is the person's BMI

Overweight: means above a weight considered normal. A BMI of 25- 29.9 is over weight.

Obesity: means too much body fat or in other words excessively above normal weight. A BMI of 30 or more is obese.

A person becomes over weight due to taking in more calories over a given period of time than their body needs for maintenance, growth and activity. The rate at which we burn off calories is termed the metabolic rate. Our metabolic rate is often faster during periods of growth and puberty but generally steadies out during adulthood. If we are active, our metabolic rate is generally higher as we need more calories to maintain an even weight. If we have a less active life then we would need fewer calories and taking in more calories than we need would cause us to put on weight.

It has been reported that obesity causes around 30,000 death in England a year and is only beaten by smoking. Obesity increases the risks of several serious conditions including diabetes, heart disease, stroke, osteoarthritis, high blood pressure, gall stone, infertility and depression. Obesity often occurs alongside a lack of exercise and seems to contribute to cancer of the colon, breast cancer, kidney cancer, and stomach cancer. In other words, to lose weight you have to reduce the amount of calorie intake and increase your activity/exercise and stay active.

Causes of weight gain

- Over eating or food addiction
-Lack of exercise
-Stress
-Genetics- children of obese parents are more likely to become - obese than those of lean parents.
-Medications can cause weight gain such as diabetes medication, - anti-depressants, psychotics, steroids and birth control medication.
-Financial difficulties where people can't afford to eat healthy foods for example fish, meat, vegetables, fruit because they are expensive where as processed fatty food is cheaper.
-Illnesses that affect weight like polycystic ovarian syndrome, hypothyroidism
-Stop smoking- a person regains their appetite because of increase in smell and taste senses after quitting smoking.
-Age- the older you get the slower your metabolism as you become less active. Menopause in women also causes weight gain.
-Pregnancy- women who are expecting gain weight to support the baby's growth- many women get back to their pre-pregnancy weight but some women struggle with their post pregnancy weight.
-Lack of sleep- losing sleep tends to make people eat more and gain weight. Lack of sleep slows the metabolism down drastically which causes the body to use less energy hence weight gain.

The symptoms below will be noticed when a person puts on extra weight;

- Sleep difficulties.
- Joint pain
- Difficulty with physical activity
- Increased sweating
- Snoring
- Breathlessness
- Gastro-oestophageal reflux disease(acid from stomach flows into gullet)
- Polycystic ovarian disease
- Reduced life expectancy

Health risks of weight gain

Coronary Heart Disease: as your body mass index increases so does your risk of getting coronary heart disease. Extra weight can also lead to heart failure where the heart can't pump enough blood to meet your body's needs.

- High blood pressure
- Stroke
- Type 2 diabetes
- Cancer: risk of colon, breast, endometrial and gall bladder cancers.
- Osteoarthritis: a common joint problem of the knees and lower back, extra weight puts more pressure on joints causing pain.
- Sleep Apnea: a common disorder where you have one or more pauses in breathing while you sleep, fat stored around the neck can narrow the airways hence making it hard to breathe.
- Obesity or being over weight causes menstrual and fertility problems in women.
- Obesity increases the risk of having gallstones. This may result in an enlarged gall bladder that doesn't work well.

The best way to prevent obesity is by eating healthily and exercising regularly. The idea behind weight loss is that the person alters their life style to a healthier one and this becomes a habit for them instead of their previous more destructive ways.

In our society, body image is very important, if we feel attractive generally we have a higher self-esteem, although many people would not consider themselves as attractive also maintain a high self-esteem. Our self-esteem should come from within rather than from the outside but the influence of external factors throughout our lives often means that we find this inner confidence hard to express.

Self- help tips for weight loss

- Eat a healthy balanced diet – three meals a day, plenty of fruit, vegetables and water remember that skipping meals will only make you hungrier. Cut down on sugar, salt and fat.
- Exercise daily, be active and stay active.
- Sleep at least 7-8 hours a night.
- Mind fitness is crucial and plays a big role in weight loss, find ways to calm and relax your mind for instance relaxation techniques, yoga, meditation, calming music whatever works for you.
- Positivity, motivation and patience will take you a long way its not going to be easy you require both mental and physical strength but with perseverance and determination you will achieve your desired goal.
- Losing weight should not be based on deprivation- DON'T starve yourself as this will shut down your metabolism, it also makes you dizzy and tired, you should not give up things but to re-assess your eating and programming your sub-conscious into eating healthy which includes taking pride in your body and looking after it.
- It is about identifying and accepting where you are going wrong, and why and then deciding to change those habits.
- Identifying where the habit comes from and which in turn helps you to understand the situation and stop blaming yourself.

WEIGHT LOSS SCRIPT

I will make myself as comfortable as I can .... take a nice deep breath ...... close my eyes and begin to relax .... just thinking about relaxing every muscle in my body ...... from the top of my head to the tips of my toes ...... As I begin to focus attention on my breathing ...... my awareness of everything around me will decrease ...... all the muscles in my body are relaxing ...... as I concentrate on breathing in and out .... I am drifting into a deeper and deeper level of relaxation ...... I am feeling lighter and lighter ...... floating higher and higher into a deeper level of relaxation .... I am now completely relaxed ...... more relaxed than I have ever felt before ..... as I experience this beautiful feeling of peace and calm .... I will completely let go of my mind ..... drift, relax and drift ...... my mind is calm, peaceful and relaxed and my whole body is completely and deeply relaxed ......

Now I am imagining myself in my special place ...... I am feeling calm and relaxed here ..... this is a very special place for me ...... I can feel it ...... I am at peace here ...... with no one to disturb me ...... this is my special time ...... my body is relaxing ..... deeper and deeper..... my mind is calm and enjoying these positive feelings .....I am feeling lighter and lighter..... floating into a comfortable relaxation ......

Because I am now at peace and relaxed ...... I can be successful at reaching my goal of losing weight ..... I am going to lose weight and become healthier and thinner ..... beginning right now by relaxing and allowing myself to accept all the suggestions ...... I imagine losing the amount of weight that I no longer want and that I will maintain that weight loss. I feel and think of myself as slimmer, thinner and healthier ..... my subconscious will now act on this image and make this image a reality ...... and now I will allow myself to lose weight ..... lose the amount of weight that I longer want and to maintain that weight loss ...... I change my bad eating patterns into good patterns now ..... and choose to become active and exercise everyday to attain my weight loss...... to be a healthy weight starting from now ...... I allow this to take place easily ...... and now I imagine a table ..... a table in front of me ..... and I fill this table with foods that are harmful to me ...... foods that make me gain weight ..... foods that are harmful to my body and mind ..... I imagine these foods; they are sweets, cakes, biscuits, crisps, doughnuts, burgers, chips, junk snacks, and fizzy drinks. I place them on the table ...... these foods are all harmful to me ..... full of calories .... useless empty calories ...... these foods are poison to my body..... these kinds of food cause me to gain weight I no longer want ...... If I choose to eat any of these foods I eat a small, small amount ...... a very tiny amount of these foods satisfies me completely ...... and now I push these foods off the table ...... I push them away from me ...... my body rejects these foods ...... my mind rejects these foods ...... I clear the table ...... and on that empty table I place the many healthy foods that I enjoy .... good healthy foods ..... foods that contain fewer calories such as vegetables, fruits, fresh bread, fresh fish, lean meat, nuts, dairy products, herbs and spices ..... the smell fills me with energy, with life and health .... and I can imagine eating all these healthy foods .... and I eat slowly and slowly .... I am are aware of the amount of food I am eating ...... and I eat modest portions and then stop ..... and that feels fine .... even with the modest portions I have eaten I feel completely satisfied ...... my whole body feels energised and I see all the many possibilities to eat healthily .... I feel lighter and more energised ...... and now I imagine seeing myself on my holiday so happy ...... thinner, healthier, stomach flat, hips and thighs firm and trim, legs firm and slim ..... I look great and feel good ..... all my friends think I look wonderful ..... and they are so happy for me ......

Food is less and less important to me ..... and whenever I think of eating I choose those good healthy foods ...... and I eat the correct amount ..... and when I eat the correct amount I stop eating ..... I simply stop eating ..... and relax ...... I am more motivated now than ever before to create the most healthy and positive life for myself ..... to change my old bad eating patterns into good new eating patterns ..... to lose the amount of weight I want to lose and to maintain this weight loss ..... I will enjoy being energetic and fit ...... and I will feel more happier, confident and healthier ...... these new habits will make permanent weight loss possible ...... from this moment on ..... I no longer have the urge to overeat or to snack in between meals .... because healthy, well balanced meals, satisfy my appetite ..... and the taste and fragrance of food are better than ever before ...... I imagine myself exercising everyday ...... burning all those calories my body doesn't need ...... and reaching my ideal weight .... I look amazing ...... I feel good and very confident ..... I look very healthy and happy .... this is me and who I want to be ..... I feel good inside and out .... and I am proud of myself ....

I will continue to enjoy my special place for another moment, experience it ...... drift and float .... I am feeling calm and relaxed.

In a few minutes I will come back to awareness ..... I will count from one to ten and as I count from one to ten I will begin to come back to full awareness .... I will come back feeling calm and relaxed ....

1.................... I am beginning to come back

2.................... All the background noises are coming back again

3 ....I am able to recall the room I'm in

4.................... I am feeling calm and completely relaxed

5 ....I am aware of my whole body

6 ....Feeling calm and peaceful

7 ....I am aware of my surroundings and all the background noises

8 ....Feeling so calm and relaxed

9 ....I am beginning to open my eyes now

10 ....I come back feeling relaxed

WEIGHT LOSS AFFIRMATIONS

- I feel great and I look great.
- I am in control of what I eat.
- I love the foods that keep me healthy.
- I look and feel lighter with each passing day.
- I can feel myself getting thinner and healthier every day.

- I enjoy the process of being healthy and losing weight.
- Everyday I get closer to my ideal weight.
- Maintaining my ideal weight is easy and effortless.
- I enjoy living a healthy and active life.
- I am fit, attractive and healthy.
- I am the healthiest I have ever been.
- I am in control of my body.
- I am extremely confident in myself.
- Losing weight comes naturally to me.
- Being thin and healthy suits me.
- Everyday I get slimmer and healthier.
- I feel great and look great in my clothes.
- I love and appreciate my body.
 -Exercising comes naturally for me and I enjoy it.
- I love my body and take good care of it.
- I am slimmer, fit and healthy and I will stay slim, fit and healthy.
- I eat slowly and stop eating the moment I am full
- I avoid eating fried foods. All the oil that my body needs is
   obtained from natural and organic foods.
- I enjoy eating small portions of food and drink lots of water
- I have eliminated sugar from my food. I now eat only nutritious
   food.
- I love eating lots of vegetables and fruits.
- I now crave for only health foods-junk food makes me sick
- I eat only when I am hungry
- Healthy eating is a way of life and comes easily to me
- I am in total control of what I eat. I only eat healthy food

···················

Chapter Six
Stress Management

Stress is the feeling of being under extreme mental or emotional pressure. Stress is a normal physical response to events that make a person feel threatened or upsets their balance in some way. When a person senses danger the body's defences kick into high mode in a rapid automatic process know as "fight or flight" mode or stress response. The stress response is the body's way of protecting it. But beyond a certain point, stress stops being helpful and starts causing major damage to health, mood, productivity, relationships and quality of life.

We all deal with stress but in different ways, stress is not an illness but it affects the way we feel, think and behave and if not addressed it can cause serious illness. Long term exposure to stress can lead to serious health problems, chronic stress disrupts nearly every system in the body, it raises blood pressure, suppresses the immune system, increases the risk of heart attack and stroke, contributes to infertility and speeds up the ageing process. Long-term stress can even rewire the brain leading to more vulnerability to anxiety and depression. Recognising the signs of stress will help you find ways of coping and dealing with it and preventing serious complications. Stress affects the mind, body and behaviour in many ways, this can be physical, emotional, cognitive and behavioural. The signs of stress are:

- Aches and pain
- Diarrhoea
- Nausea
- Constipation
- Dizziness
- Chest pain
- Rapid heart beat
- Loss of sex drive

- Frequent colds
- Moodiness
- Irritability or short temper
- Agitation
- Inability to relax
- Sense of loneliness
- Depression or general unhappiness
- Memory problems
- Inability to concentrate
- Poor judgement
- Negativity
- Anxiety/racing thoughts
- Feeling overwhelmed
- Isolation
- Eating more or less
- Sleeping too much or too little
- Neglecting responsibilities
- Constant worrying
- Using alcohol, drugs, cigarettes to relax
- Nervous habits such as nail biting and pacing

The causes of stress are both internal and external with the internal factors being psychological problems such as worry, fear, guilt, frustration, anxiety and the external factors being work, relationships, family, finances and health among others.

Self-help for managing stress

- Understand what is stressing you and take steps to deal with the situation rather than ignoring it because it will not go away until you address it.

- Have plenty of rest and sleep for a healthy balance for both your body and mind.

- Take time to exercise as exercise produces hormones that induce positive feelings.

- Use of breathing and relaxation techniques will help to calm your mind. (Chapter Two)

- Avoid people and situations that cause you stress.

- Check and re-assess your diet- a healthy balanced diet is very important and avoid toxins like drugs, alcohol, nicotine and also cut down on caffeine as these substances create imbalance in your body and increase stress levels.

- Talk to someone, a problem shared is a problem halved. If you feel that it's all too much and you're not coping then seek advice from your doctor.

Self- hypnosis is the most valuable exercise for control of stress. Self-hypnosis for stress revolves around helping you to learn to relax and also to learn some triggers that will assist you to deal with the physical symptoms of the condition, which in turn will enable you to make physical changes that you need to make in your life. The hypnosis script should be used twice a day at least until full effectiveness is achieved.

STRESS MANAGEMENT SCRIPT

I will make myself as comfortable as I can ...... take a nice deep breath ...... close my eyes and begin to relax ...... just thinking about relaxing every muscle in my body ..... from the top of my head to the tips of my toes ...... as I begin to focus attention on my breathing ...... my awareness of everything around me will decrease ..... I let all the muscles in my face relax ...... around my eyes and as I concentrate on relaxing this area every muscle in my body will relax ...... I am drifting into a deeper and deeper level of relaxation ...... feeling heavy ...... like a heavy weight being lifted off my shoulders ...... I am feeling lighter and lighter ..... floating higher and higher into a deeper level of relaxation .... I am now completely relaxed .... more relaxed than I have ever felt before .... completely relaxed from the top of my head to my toes .... my mind is calm and relaxed ...... drifting and floating ...... as I experience this beautiful feeling of peace and calm ...... I will let go completely .... drifting, relaxing and drifting .....

Now that I am completely relaxed ...... I am imagining myself in my special place ...... feeling relaxed more deeply relaxed than I have ever felt before .... I begin to concentrate on how my body is feeling ..... how my mind is feeling .... no one wants anything from me .... no this time its just me ...... now I give myself permission to completely let go of all worry and tension ...... to let it happen .... my body feels free ...... and lighter ...... my muscles feel released ....yet stronger .... I concentrate on my muscles that have a tendency to feel tense ....feeling how they are at the moment ...... I feel at peace .... deeply relaxed and ready to deal with the day more effectively .... I notice that my breathing is slower .... stable .... deeper .... this feeling is so much better .... so much more at peace and relaxed .... Now I go on to notice how my mind feels .... relaxed and totally stress free .... that constant interfering noise has left ...... that irritating noise has left my mind there is no longer room for it .... my mind now is free .... and for a while I am going to let it drift ...... and drift .... let it think of gentle peaceful things .... positive things ...... good times that I have had in the past ...... happy times .... lovely times that I wish to have in the future .... no unpleasant thoughts are allowed in my mind when I am in this state and if they try .... which is so very unlikely then I can just push them away .... in this relaxed and calm state of my mind ...... my subconscious will accept all the suggestions and new ways of dealing with stress ...... as it hears everything and always pays attention ..... and it is my subconscious mind that I am talking to right now ....Now as my mind is at peace my body is so at peace .... I will just let go of myself and become open to the changes that I want to make in my life .... from this day forward ..... with my powerful imagination I can see and feel just how I would like my life to be .... I know now how important it is to spend time relaxing .... how much clearer everything becomes .....how much free ..... how much more motivated I can feel and above all how much better I feel now that I have found this special way of letting the stress go out of my life

.... more and more I am realising that I have control over the stress that I feel .... I can let it go .... I can let it go .... I have made my body and mind feel like this ...... and I can do it again and again ..... and be so much less stressed .... less confused .... and so very much more in control .... more at ease ......

Now that I have learnt how to relax I can appreciate how good it feels and how much my body and mind need to experience this feeling and how very much better everything feels when I have reached this inner feeling of calm ......I will enjoy my special place for another moment ..... experience it ..... drift and float ..... I am feeling calm and relaxed ......

In a few minutes I will come back to awareness ...... I will count from one to ten .... and as I count from one to ten I will begin to come back to full awareness ..... I will come back feeling relaxed.

1....................Begin to come back
2....................
3 ....Feeling relaxed
4....................
5 ....Calm and peaceful
6 ....
7 ....Feeling relaxed
8 ....I am aware of the normal surroundings now
9 ....I begin to open my eyes now
10 ....I open my eyes and come back feeling wonderful

STRESS AFFIRMATIONS

- I can see stressful situations as challenges
- Challenges bring opportunities
- I can choose a positive frame of mind
- I can handle whatever comes my way
- I am in control of how I feel.
- I am in control of how I react to challenging situations
- I can create inner peace
- I am strong and capable
- Stress is leaving my body

- Stress is a thing in the past
- I breath in peace
- My mind is calm
- My body is at peace
- I release all tension from my body and mind
- I have started to notice how calm and relaxed I am
- I am relaxed and free from stress
- Everyday I become more and more peaceful and content
- Releasing stress is becoming easier
- I am stress free
- My life feels more balanced and enjoyable
- I live a calm, healthy and relaxed life style and that suits me
- I am in control
- I let go of all the negativity that rests in my body and mind
- I am calm, at peace and stress free
- My body and mind are at peace
- I am stress free

****

Chapter Seven
Depression

Depression is a state of low mood and aversion to activity that can affect a person's thoughts, behaviour, feelings and sense of well being. Depression causes sadness, anxiety, emptiness, hopelessness, worthlessness, guilty feelings, irritability, anger, and hurt.

Depression can also be looked at as a defence mechanism that a body adopts in order to escape from distress. Depression can affect anyone from different age groups, sexes, and cultures, it is very common. If it's mild most people can lead a normal healthy life with the right treatment and support, however if it's severe it can be devastating and also become life threatening or even cause death. A depressed person looses interest in activities that once were pleasurable, experiences loss of appetite or over eating. A depressed mood is not necessarily a psychiatric order. It may be a normal reaction to certain life events, a symptom to some medical conditions, or a side effect of some drugs or medical treatments. Spotting the signs early and getting help is vital. It's important to seek help from your doctor if you think you may be depressed, many people wait a long time before seeking help, and it's advisable to seek help sooner and the sooner the recovery.

The symptoms of depression

- Feelings of sadness
- Irritability or frustration
- Loss of interest in normal activities
- Reduced sex drive
- Insomnia or excessive sleeping
- Loss of appetite or excessive eating
- Weight loss or weight gain
- Agitation or restlessness
- Slowed thinking, speaking, body movements

- Anger
- Decreased concentration
- Fatigue, tiredness, loss of energy
- Crying spells for no apparent reason
- Suicide thoughts
- Unexplained physical problems for example back pain or headaches

Causes of depression

It's not known exactly what causes depression. As with many mental illnesses, other factors may be involved in its cause.

- Biological differences; People with depression appear to have physical changes in their brains.
- Neurotransmitters; These naturally occurring brain chemicals linked to mood are thought to play a direct role in depression.
- Hormones; Changes in the body's balance of hormones may be involved in causing or triggering depression.
- Inherited traits/Hereditary; Depression is more common in people whose biological family members also have this condition.
- Life events; such as death, divorce, financial problems, childbirth, illness, high stress can also trigger depression in some people.
- Early childhood trauma; Traumatic events during childhood such as abuse or loss of parents may cause permanent changes in the brain that make you more susceptible to depression.
-

Self-help tips for depression

- Eat a healthy balanced diet
- Exercise regularly- get out and be active go for a walk or a run and shake off all the negativity and low moods. Keeping active lifts your moods and fills you with positivity.
- Have plenty of sleep and rest
- Relaxation techniques will help you calm and relax your mind (Chapter Two)
- Avoid the use of drugs, alcohol, tobacco
- Meditation and yoga are also a great way to relax your mind and calm you down

- Join a self-help group where you can discuss your feelings and concerns with other sufferers and also sharing experiences and coping strategies.
- Make time to do the things that you enjoy doing such as socialising with friends, family, taking part in your favourite sport or activities.
- Be positive and stay around positive people who will help lift your moods

Hypnosis and deep relaxation techniques are a very effective and versatile tool for treating depression. Clinical depression is one of the most prevalent mental health problem today. If you are clinically depressed you need help as living with depression is a daily struggle. Life is too short to be depressed. When people are depressed they don't think clearly. They hold a pessimistic view of the future, unrealistic expectations and are overly critical of themselves.

Depression causes negative thoughts and private self-talk that perpetuates your negative feelings and predicament. Self-hypnosis can interrupt this process because negative thoughts repeated over and over again become imprinted in your subconscious mind. This is where hypnosis can be helpful in offering a positive way of thinking your way out of a negative predicament. Through self-hypnosis, the doorway to your subconscious mind is opened with use of positive suggestions to;

- Change your negative self-suggestions
- Reduce your feelings of guilt and self-blame
- Help you to begin making positive choices again

DEPRESSION SCRIPT

I will make myself as comfortable as I can .... I will take a nice deep breath in ..... close my eyes ...... and begin to relax ...... just thinking about relaxing every muscle in my body ...... from the top of my head to the tips of my toes ...... as I begin to focus attention on my breathing ...... my awareness of everything around me will decrease.

I let all the muscles in my face relax ..... starting with muscles around my eyes and as I concentrate on relaxing this area every muscle in my body will relax ..... I will then let the muscles around my jaws and mouth relax .... feeling limp and loose as my lips part slightly letting go of all the tension .... this relaxation spreads to my shoulders and neck .... then to my arms and back ...... relaxing all those muscles completely .... now I notice the same feeling moving into my abdomen ...... to my thighs and legs .... past my knees, ankles feet and into my toes ...... soothing, calming and relaxing all my body .... as I continue to breath in and out slowly .... I relax even more and more drifting into a deeper and deeper level of relaxation ...... I am feeling lighter and lighter ..... floating higher and higher into a deeper level of relaxation ..... I am now completely relaxed .... more relaxed than I have ever felt before ......as I experience this beautiful feeling of peace and calm .... I let go of my mind .... drifting ...... relaxing .... and drifting ......

Now I am imagining myself in my special place .... this is a very special place for me .... I can feel it and see it in my mind .... feeling my body relax .... deeper and deeper...... enjoying these positive feelings .... I am feeling lighter and lighter..........floating higher and higher into a comfortable relaxation ....

Because I am now relaxed I let any feelings I have buried come up to the surface ..... I now allow the emotions that are arising within me pass right through me ....sadness, anger, disappointment or guilt ...... I am letting all my emotions surface and float to the top. Feelings of fear .... loss .... resentment .... I let them all float and surface to the top ...... there is no need for me to resist I let my body relax and as I drift into a deeper relaxation ...... I let myself forgive all the things I have blamed ..... I forgive each person ...... I forgive myself .... I feel a compassion enter my heart ..... I let go of all the anger, sadness and pain I have been feeling ..... I let it pass ...... I am feeling it pass through me and out of me .... and as I let these emotions go I feel a new sense of peace emerge ...... I know I am alright ..... I know I can make it and I know I can do it ...... I know I have the courage to move ahead beyond my loss ..... my body and spirit will heal ..... each day I grow stronger ..... healing and recovering ...... healing and recovering ...... I am drifting and floating in a warm glow of healing energy ...... there is no need to resist .... drifting ...... floating and relaxing.

Depression is a healing process so I can allow myself to mourn or be sad .... and when I have completed the time of sadness .... I will set myself free ..... I am good to myself and the time will soon be over for those feelings ..... and I will feel free from them ..... I will feel free .... because I can accept and get rid of any feelings ...... discard any feelings I am through with ...... they are mine ...... I can let them come and go ...... come and go as I go through them ...... now I will continue to relax .... feeling myself relax with my feelings .... and think of how I am a whole person with many feelings that make me whole and healthy ...... and if any unwanted out side pressure comes at me ...... I will be surrounded by a shield that protects me from pressure ...... this shield will protect me from the pressure ...... the shield prevents outside pressure from invading me...... pressure bounces off and away from me ..... bounces off and away ...... no matter where it comes from or who sends it .... it bounces off and away ...... and I feel fine because the shield protects me all day from any stress, harm and pressure ...... I go through my day feeling fine ...... I watch the stress bounce off and away ...... filling me with calmness inside ...... calm inside ...... I am a calm person and I am shielded from stress ..... I act in ways that make me feel good ..... I now have new responses to old situations ..... from now on when I think about situations that bring me sadness, pain and stress ......I will not feel anxious, sad, guilty, resentful, angry or disappointed .... I will rather breath deeply and feel love, happiness, compassion, forgiveness and peace .... feeling calm and relaxed .... this new response will make me feel strong, calm and free ...... my days will be full of accomplishments and I will be pleased with those accomplishments .... I will feel good about myself because I have new responses that are making my day more pleasant ...... I am calm, strong and free from stress and depression .... I am completely free of stress ......

I will continue to enjoy my special place for another moment ....
experience it .... and relax .... until I am ready to come back to
full awareness ...... and when I am ready to come back I will count
from one to five ...... and as count to five I will open my eyes and
come back feeling relaxed and at peace ....

1.................... Beginning to come back
2.................... Coming up
3.................... Feeling relaxed
4.................... Beginning to open your eyes
5.................... I open my eyes and come back all the way feeling
                      wonderful

DEPRESSION AFFIRMATIONS

I find it easy to stay positive
- I only focus on positive things in my life
- I am happy
- I am free of depression
- I am free of negative thoughts
- I am happy with who I am
- I have a strong mind
- I find it easy to think only positive thoughts
- I find it easy to stay happy
- I will beat depression
- Everyday I feel less depressed
- Each day I feel happier
- I will be free of negativity
- I will only focus on the best of life
- I will only think positive thoughts
- I am in control of my thoughts
- Beating depression has made me a stronger person
- I have over come depression
- I am happy and content with who I am
- My possibilities are endless
- I feel good inside and out
- I love myself
- I am stress free

- I am at peace
- The best is yet to come into my life
- Everyday good things come to me
- I forgive the past and move into a positive future
- I am in the flow of love
- I feel stronger each day
- I am free of depression
- I am in control of my life

....

Chapter Eight
Anxiety

Anxiety is the feeling or more correctly the set of feelings that we get when we feel apprehension or fear. We can feel anxiety when we are subjected to long-term stress or when we feel threatened by something or someone. We can also experience anxiety when we are not aware of what we are feeling anxious about. How we respond to stress is in some ways inherited from our parents and will also depend on the environment we live in.

Anxiety or a tendency towards it is also inherited in the fact that some people are more susceptible to feelings of anxiety than others. We all feel anxious at some point in our lives and this is a normal instinctual response that serves as a protection to aid survival. It teaches us to avoid dangerous situations, this way anxiety is a learning process. This works very well in obvious situations like being mugged or attacked where we will run or fight back defensively depending on what seems to be the best option.

Anxiety will affect our whole being, our emotions, our behaviour and our physical health. It primarily creates feelings of fear that make us want to avoid situations that it is trying to get us to avoid. We will often make anxiety worse by persistently thinking negative thoughts that increase our feelings of anxiety. Due to the feelings that anxiety creates in us, it is a cyclical process whereby the more anxious we feel, the more anxious we become and hence the more negative we feel, which then creates a greater need to avoid things that make us feel anxious. Anxiety therefore can be a precursor to depression.

Anxiety becomes abnormal if it persists even when the stressful situation has gone or if it appears for no reason and if it interferes with your everyday life. Although feeling anxious can be normal , you should seek help from your doctor if it affects your life and causes you extreme distress. Anxiety can be accompanied by physical symptoms which include;

- Trembling,
- Tense muscles
- Churning stomach
- Nausea
- Diarrhoea
- Headaches
- Backache
- Heart palpitations
- Numbness
- Sweating or flushing

Causes of anxiety

- Stressful life changing events such as divorce, childbirth, bereavement, home move
- Mental health problems like depression
- Physical illness
- Drug use
- Medication side effects or drug withdrawal
- Work, school, exams, tests
- Financial difficulties
- Anxiety can be hereditary or run in families

Self-help tips for anxiety

- Deep breathing and relaxation exercises keep your mind calm as mental coping is the focus and strongest tool in managing anxiety. (Chapter Two)
- Exercise
- Eat healthily
- Plenty of sleep
- Avoid alcohol, drugs, nicotine and over using over-the-counter drugs, they may provide a short term relief but will do more damage in the long run and in return will make you even more anxious than before.

Self-hypnosis can help you control the mind to stop anxiety. It can be accomplished in many ways, but it is consistently based upon the principles trying to change the beliefs and mental associations that causes you to think and act the way you do. Anxiety often occurs due to a person's negative associations or negative beliefs around particular situations, settings and objects. Self-hypnosis can be a useful tool for controlling these negative feelings and beliefs and thus controlling anxiety.

ANXIETY SCRIPT

I will make myself as comfortable as I can .... take a nice deep breath .... close my eyes and begin to relax .... and just think about relaxing every muscle in my body .... from the top of my head to the tips of my toes .... as I begin to focus attention on my breathing .... my awareness of everything around me will decrease .... with every breath I take .... I relax even more and more .... I inhale and exhale .... letting all the muscles in my face and around my eyes relax ...... and as I concentrate on relaxing this area the relaxation flows to my mouth and jaw .... letting all the tightness and tension leave my body and loosening me up ...... this relaxation travels to my neck and shoulders smoothing all those muscles out .... completely relaxing them ...... I then relax my chest, back and hands .... completely relaxing each muscle with every breath I take in and out ...... this sensation flows down to my stomach, thighs and leg muscles loosening them and relaxing them ...... and then to my ankles, feet and toes .... every muscle in my body feels completely relaxed now .... I drift into a deeper and deeper level of relaxation .... feeling lighter and lighter .... floating higher and higher into a deeper level of relaxation .... I am now completely relaxed .... more relaxed than I have ever felt before .... as I experience this feeling of peace and calm .... I let go of my mind .... drifting and floating .... relaxing ....

Now that I am in a comfortable state of relaxation .... I am imagining myself in my special place .... this is a very special place for me .... I can feel it .... it's calm, peaceful and relaxing and I am feeling my entire body and mind completely at ease and relaxed here .... deeper and deeper........ enjoying these tranquil positive feelings ...... I am feeling lighter and lighter..........floating higher and higher into a comfortable relaxation ...... I feel wonderful .... and blissfully happy .... I let myself drift deeper and deeper ......

Because I am feeling relaxed .... more deeply relaxed than I have ever felt before ..... I feel safe and secure ...... I am aware now that the symptoms of anxiety are my body's natural fight or flight response ...... they are natural and harmless ..... sometimes during our lives we learn to be stressed, nervous, anxious .... because of our insecurities .... the numerous challenges ...... bad experiences .... feelings of inferiority ...... being fearful ..... or maybe because we have traumas from the past ...... but whatever my symptoms .... I know that they are unimportant and that I am medically safe ...... my symptoms are natural I am losing my fear of the symptoms of anxiety .... I am becoming stronger and more confident ......I am in control of my fears and anxieties ...... my subconscious mind knows and has the answers .... it has the means of healing .... my mind is healing right now .... as my deepest and biggest emotional injuries will be located and my mind will be able to cure any problem .... any conflict .... any pain .... any worries .... fears ...... and that's why right now I am feeling calm and relaxed .... and as that feeling is increasing my mind is finding and solving all the problems .... one by one ...... every fear .... conflict .... pain .... injury .... anxiety ...... from now on I will control my feelings ...... and my emotions ...... and I will not be worried about anything .... there will be only calm and peace .... I will be strong and in control .... I can relax my body whenever I feel fear ..... I will take a deep breath in and out and the anxiety will pass as quickly as It arrived ...... my anxiety will pass quickly ...... it passes in less that two minutes when I empty my mind of anxious thoughts .... when I am feeling anxious and fearful I can stop the anxious thoughts ...... stop the thoughts of fear ..... Inside my mind I will shout "STOP"! to the anxious thoughts ...... knowing that my fear will stop in less than two minutes ..... it will stop .... I will be strong and firm .... now I know how to shake off the anxiety, fear and everything I worry about .... my mind and my feelings are calm ...... Now that I have new responses to my old anxiety ..... I no longer frighten myself with fears .... I am letting go of the anxiety .... letting go of it .... letting go of my fears ...... now that I have learned new ways to deal with my anxiety and fears .... I feel strong ...... healthier .... and calmer .... and as I go on everyone will be amazed with this new person full of tranquillity and deep inner peace .... and from now on I be able to go into situations where I once felt anxious ...... I can cope with my feelings .... I go wherever I want to go and I do whatever I want to do because I am confident in my ability to cope ..... I have new abilities to cope and I feel a growing confidence in my abilities to cope ...... I am in control and able to cope in any challenging situation .... with confidence, in control and relaxed ....

I will enjoy my special place for another moment ...... take all the positive feelings in ...... and bring them back with me ..... and I will notice that as soon as I open my eyes .... I will feel a deeply calm ...... a feeling that will increase every single day ....

When I am ready to come back to full alertness I will count ..... I will count from one to ten and as I count from one to ten I will begin to come back to full awareness ...... and I will come back feeling calm and relaxed ......

1.................... Beginning to come back
2.................... The background noises are coming back
3 .... I am feeling relaxed
4.................... I am aware of my body
5 ....Calm and peaceful
6 ....I am almost fully alert now
7 ....Feeling relaxed
8 ....I am aware of the normal surroundings now
9 ....I am begin to open my eyes now
10 ....I open my eyes and come back feeling wonderful

ANXIETY AFFIRMATIONS

I am free of anxiety and continue to do so I am always safe and protected

- I am free of fear
- I release all fears. I am free.
- Life will always provide for me
- All is well and calm
- I am a strong and capable human being
- I am in control of my emotions
- I am in control of my life
- No person has any power over me
- I am always safe and guided by my higher self
- I release, I relax, I let go
- I am calm and relaxed
- My anxiety does not control me
- I have a great life and will continue to do so
- I have power over my anxiety
- I am a worthy and deserving human being
- My mind is relaxed and at peace
- Letting go of worry and fear is getting easier and easier
- I deserve to relax and stop worrying
- I am in control of the way I react in stressful situations
- Freeing myself from stress and anxiety makes me healthier and happier
- I am breaking free of anxiety
- Anxiety is in my past

....

Chapter Nine
Panic Attacks

A panic attack is a sudden wave of extreme anxiety and fear causing the sufferer to experience heart pounding, breathlessness and even feel as if they are out of control and dying. Panic attacks cause acute anxiety reactions and sometimes they come with no apparent reason or warning. Their cause is not clear. Panic attacks usually last between five to twenty minutes but for some people they come in waves that may last for two hours. It can be very stressful living with panic attacks and many sufferers go on to develop further problems such as depression, drug and or alcohol abuse.

Panic attacks are related to slight abnormalities in brain messenger chemicals known as neurotransmitters, which is the reason why medications can be effective in their relief. Like stress and anxiety, panic attacks tend to run in families and can be triggered by life crises like bereavement, divorce, accidents, illness among others.

According to the American Psychiatric Associations Official Diagnostic & Statistical Manual of Mental Health Disorders IV(DSM-IV) In order for a panic attack to be diagnosed, the sufferer has to display at least four of the following symptoms:

Palpitations, pounding heart or rapid heart rate
- Sweating
- Trembling and shaking
- Feelings of Choking
- Sensations of shortness of breath
- Nausea and abdominal distress
- Chest pain and discomfort
- Feeling dizzy, unsteady or faint
- Detachment from one self
- Fear of losing control
- Fear of dying

- Numbness or tingling sensations
- Chills or hot flushes

As with many mental health conditions the exact cause of panic attacks is not fully understood. It is thought that it is probably caused by a combination of physical and psychological factors. If you have the symptoms of panic attacks see your doctor. A diagnosis will be made for you if you experience recurrent and un expected panic attacks.

The main aim of treatment for panic attacks is to reduce the number of attacks that you have and to help ease the severity of symptoms. Self-hypnosis helps with panic attacks by enabling a more relaxed state. Hypnosis can help alleviate panic attacks by direct suggestion and by behavioural training it can also be useful in the following;

- Learning new ways to relax
- Break habitual behaviours
- Remove anxiety triggers
- Help take back control by recognising and regulating inappropriate responses
- Dissociate the sufferer from anxiety causing problems

Panic attack self-help tips

- Practice relaxation and breathing techniques as this will help promote relaxation and also increase feelings of calmness and inner peace. Find a quiet place everyday to practice. (Chapter Two)
- Avoid smoking and caffeine because they provoke panic attacks.
- Find information and learn all you need to know about the condition and how to deal with it.
- Join a support group where you can share your feelings with others in similar circumstances and understand what you are going through.
- If you feel overwhelmed and can't cope anymore don't suffer in silence seek advice from your doctor.

PANIC ATTACK SCRIPT

I will make myself as comfortable as I can, take a nice deep breath, close my eyes and begin to relax, just think about relaxing every muscle in my body, from the top of my head to the tips of my toes .... As I begin to focus attention on my breathing .... my awareness of everything around me will decrease .... I will let all the muscles in my body relax ..... I will concentrate on relaxing every muscle in my body and my breathing .... relaxing completely .... I notice the rate of my breathing slowing down ...... and that every time I breath in and out I relax even more and more ...... I am beginning to let go of all the tension in my body .... and relaxing my entire body even more ...... I am drifting deeper and deeper into a comfortable relaxation .... I feel lighter and lighter .... floating higher and higher .... I am completely relaxed ...... more relaxed than I have ever felt before ......as I experience this beautiful feeling of peace and calm ...... I will let go of my mind .... drifting ....relaxing .... and drifting .... now that I am deeply relaxed and feeling safe .... I will imagine my special place .... it's a very special place for me .... just for me .... I feel safe and at peace in my special place ...... I can see it ...... and can feel it .... I am feeling my body relax even more here .... no one wants anything from me .... its my time .... its all about me .... no stress ...... no fear ...... no worries .... no anxiety ...... it's total peace and tranquil .... I will enjoy these positive feelings .... I am feeling lighter and lighter .... floating higher and higher into a comfortable relaxation .... I feel wonderful inside and out ......

Because this is my choice ..... this is my decision to make this important change in my life ...... I will find it easy ...... with the benefit of my subconscious mind .... with the full support of and understanding of the deeper part of my mind to .... eliminate my panic attacks .... until now I have been experiencing these uncomfortable feelings .... feelings of unsettled emotions .... feelings of discomfort and anxiety .... feelings of panic .... feelings of fear .... which have begun to interfere with my life ...... from now on .... I am setting myself free from those fears ....

they are neither useful, desirable or appropriate ...... they are frightening .... they are alarming .... and detrimental to my health .... From now on I will relax my body whenever I feel fear or panic .... I will breath deeply ...... deeply .... pushing the air into my abdomen .... deep down into my belly .... and slowly letting go .... whenever I feel anxious I will begin taking slow deep breaths .... I will relax my whole body .... I will let my shoulders drop and relax .... I will let my jaw hang loosely and relax .... I will let my forehead loosen up and relax .... I will relax any tension in my body .... Now I have the tools and knowledge to let go of anxiety and fear .....

I know now that panic passes quickly when I stop my anxious thoughts .... it passes quickly when I empty my mind of anxious thoughts .... and very soon it will be over .... when I feel anxious .... I will stop the anxious thoughts .... the self destructive thoughts ...... inside my mind I will shout STOP .... and they will stop .... and the panic will stop ...... it will be over .... I am in charge now .... I am in control and have the ability to release all panic and anxious thoughts .... Now that I have new responses to my old anxious thoughts ...... I will no longer frighten myself with the fears .... I am letting go of my old fears .... anxiety .... panic ...... I am letting go .... right now I remind myself of my new responses to my old anxious thoughts .... those thoughts are fading .... fading away .... fading away ....I know now that I can accept any feelings in my body .... I know they are just passing .... just passing like the wind ...... and soon will be gone ...... my anxiety and panic will soon be gone .... I am feeling stronger and stronger ...... more and more confident .... and more in control .... I have nothing to fear ..... I am now able to cope ...... with my feelings and can relax and cope .... and let them pass .... from now on I will be able to enter any situations that were stressful for me .... I can go wherever I want to go and do whatever I want to do with confidence .... because I am in charge now .... I am in control .... I am strong and confident .... I will enjoy my special place for as long as I want ..... when I am ready I will come back to full consciousness .... feeling stronger and more positive .... feeling confident and strong .... and then I will count from one to ten and with each number I will become more and more awake .... with beautiful feelings flowing through my body .... calm and peaceful thoughts going through my mind ...... I will wake up feeling fine .... feeling calm .... peaceful .... confident .... and relaxed ....

1 .... I am beginning to come back
2 .... All the background noises are coming back again
3 .... I am able to recall the room I am in
4 .... I am feeling calm and completely relaxed
5 .... I am aware of my whole body
6 ....I am feeling calm and peaceful
7 ....I am aware of my surroundings and all the background noises
8 ....Feeling so calm and relaxed
9 ....I begin to open my eyes now
10 ....I open my eyes and come back feeling at peace

PANIC ATTACK AFFIRMATIONS

- I am calm
- I am able to let go of panic
- I am a relaxed person
- I am in control
- I am safe and secure
- I breath easily and naturally
- I am able to mentally detach from panic attacks
- I will eliminate panic attacks
- I will stay calm under pressure
- I will always stay in control
- I will remind myself that I am safe
- I will be okay
- I am in control of my breathing
- I will maintain focus and control
- I am feeling more relaxed
- I will overcome panic attacks
- I am letting go of panic attacks

- I am in control
- I feel calm and relaxed
- I am panic free
- I am confident and strong
- My life is calm, relaxed and panic free
- I am always calm and will remain calm in tricky situations
- I am more and more in control of my panic attacks
- When I feel anxious I deeply breath in and out
- Deeply breathing in makes me feel calm and relaxed
- I am getting better each day at dealing with panic
- I am stronger than the panic attacks
- I can handle anything because I'm in charge

·················

Chapter Ten
Pain Management

Pain is defined by the International Association for Study of Pain as an unpleasant sensory and emotional experience associated with actual or potential tissue damage or described in terms of damage, medications which block pain are called analgesics; hypno-nalgesia is the use of hypnotherapy/hypnosis as an analgesic. Pain may be caused by injury, illness or surgery and its a common condition that may be anything from mild to extreme.

Pain is usually used by the body as a warning that all is not right within our physical body and sometimes more covertly in our emotional selves. Without the ability to feel pain we would be in grave danger as we would continue to damage tissue and ignore symptoms for illness which would eventually cause death. Pain is categorized into two types:

Acute Pain; This is pain that results from disease, inflammation or injury. It will generally come on suddenly and be accompanied by anxiety or emotional distress. It is treatable and defined by the fact it will have an ending and will lessen as the body heals. In some cases it can give way to chronic pain.

Chronic Pain; This type of pain persists over a longer period of time and is made worse by the environment the person is living in and their psychological state. Chronic pain is often resistant to orthodox medical treatments.

We feel pain in a variety of ways, in an ache, a prick, a burning sensation or a tingle. We can use self-hypnosis to help both types of pain (although acute pain is often helped by the person learning or having learned self-hypnosis) How hypnosis works in the treatment of pain is not yet fully understood but the fact is that it does work for some people. It is generally used to control and contain the amount of pain a person can stand. The use of relaxation techniques seems to assist in a person's ability to deal with the pain and the reduction of anxiety helps further. Hypnosis may also be useful due to the effect it may have on some chemicals working within the nervous system, the effect being that certain impulses are slowed down.

Self-help tips for pain management

- Heat or cold packs can help relieve pain, an ice pack can help reduce swelling after an injury.
- Massage works well with soft tissue and a lot of people find relief from having a massage, however massages should be avoided with joint pain.
- Relaxation and breathing techniques work well in relieving pain together with yoga and meditation. (Chapter Two)
- Acupuncture- several studies have found that acupuncture can be helpful in relieving pain for people with serious illnesses like cancer.
- If you are in extreme pain see a doctor and don't self-medicate!
-

PAIN MANAGEMENT SCRIPT

I will make myself as comfortable as I can ...... take a nice deep breath ...... close my eyes and begin to relax .... and think about relaxing every muscle in my body .... as I begin to focus attention on my breathing .... my awareness of everything around me will decrease ...... and all the background noises will fade away slowly ...... I will let all my muscles relax from the top of my head to the tips of my toes .... as I continue to gently breath in through my noise and breath out through my abdomen ...... concentrating on relaxing every muscle in my body ...... letting go of all the tension, stiffness and stress ..... smoothing and loosening all the muscles and relaxing them completely ...... I am drifting into a deeper and deeper level of relaxation ...... feeling light, light ...... like a heavy weight has been lifted off my shoulders ...... I am floating higher and higher into a deeper level of relaxation .... I notice that my breathing is slowing down more .... and the more it slows down .... the more relaxed I become ...... I am now completely relaxed .... more relaxed than I have ever felt before .... as I am

61

experiencing this beautiful feeling of peace and calm .... I will let go of my mind .... drifting .... relaxing ...... floating .... at peace ......I am imagining myself in my special place ...... this is a very special place for me ....I am feeling it ...... and all the good sensations in this place .... feeling my body relax even more .... deeper and deeper........ I notice how comfortable my body feels ..... drifting and floating ...... this is the most peaceful place in the world for me .... I am feeling a sense of peace flow through me ...... a sense of well-being ...... I take in all these positive feelings ...... feeling at peace with this relaxation ...... from now on I will be able to relax deeper and deeper .... regardless of the pain and stress in my life .... the pain will bounce off ...... the stress will bounce off ...... bouncing off as I become more and more relaxed ...... I will continue to enjoy these positive feelings .... I am feeling lighter and lighter....... my body is at rest ...... and mind is at peace ...... I am floating higher and higher into a comfortable relaxation .... I feel calm and peaceful ...... Now that I am very deeply relaxed ...... and as my body relaxes ...... so does my mind ...... and because of this I am more receptive to new ways of dealing with my pain .... new ways to cope with pain ...... everything useful that goes into my mind will become embedded there and work with me into the future ...... causing a lasting and positive impression ..... the way I behave ...... and the thoughts behind those actions ..... this effect will last beyond today ..... the things that I accept here will go with me having a positive effect on everything I do .....as my subconscious mind accepts these positive suggestions they will become a part of me ...... naturally and positively a part of me ...... Now I am focussing attention on my pain .... Imagining this pain and discomfort to be a large red ball of energy .... now I am imagining this large ball of energy become smaller and smaller .... I am imagining the colour of the ball beginning to change to a bright white colour .... and reducing in size .... becoming smaller and smaller ...... the smaller and smaller this white ball of energy becomes .... the less and less discomfort and pain I feel ...... I am feeling better as I watch the ball of light becomes lighter and lighter .... and even more better when it becomes smaller and smaller

.... I am feeling stronger and stronger ...... energised by the ball of light .... this feeling will always be mine .... and will stay with me for as long as I need it .... Imagining this ball of light will always ease my pain .... make me feel comfortable .... and at peace with myself .... as the pain melts away .... and as the ball of light disappears .... I feel even better .... more comfortable .... more relaxed .... and at peace .... and this feeling will remain with me always .... from this moment forwards I will be able to control this feeling at any time .... and it will always make me feel better .... completely relaxed ...... comfortable and at peace ....

I will continue to enjoy my special place for another moment .... experience it .... drift and float ...... feeling calm and relaxed .... calm and relaxed ......In a few minutes when I am ready to come back to full awareness .... I will count from one to five and as I count from one to five I will begin to come back .... feeling totally relaxed ...... feeling comfortable .... energized and at peace ......

1 .... I am beginning to come back
2 .... My awareness of my surroundings is coming back
3 .... I am coming up
4 .... I am feeling relaxed
5 .... I am more and more alert now
6 .... I am feeling calm and relaxed
7 .... I am feeling comfortable
8 .... All my normal sounds are back
9 .... I am beginning to open my eyes
10 .... I open my eyes and come back feeling great

PAIN MANAGEMENT AFFIRMATIONS

- I am pain free
- I give myself permission to relax
- I feel good
- I feel strong

- I release all the pain
- I choose to live pain free
- I am releasing more and more pain everyday

- My happy thoughts help to heal my healthy body
- I am grateful for my healthy body. I love life.
- I am releasing all my pain
- All my body is relaxed
- My mind is relaxed
- I am in control of my body
- Each day I feel better and better
- I let go of my tension in my body
- My body and mind are connected working towards my health
- My body has a natural ability to heal its self
- Each day I am becoming healthier and fitter
- I accept health as a natural state of my being
- I love myself
- I love my body
- I feed my body nourishing foods
- I exercise my body everyday
- I connect with the part of myself that knows how to heal
- I am pain free and totally in sync with life
- I release all my pain
- I am healthy and happy
- I am balanced and happy
- Healing is happening to my body
- I am pain free.

****

Chapter Eleven
Child Birth

Giving birth is a joyous, instinctive and fascinating process which requires physical, emotional and mental strength. It is very common that during pregnancy women become anxious and worried about giving birth. Childbirth is normally associated with pain because it is hard work and it is normal to fear for yourself and your baby. Fear is a normal part of the birthing process, however extreme fear can cause problems as it reduces contractions, placental blood flow and can also manifest itself in nightmares, breathlessness and heart palpitations. The pain that is mostly experienced during labour is reported to be caused by two main factors, these being: the physical contractions of the womb and the distension of tissues as the baby is born and the psychological coating of fear, worry and anxiety arising from expectation that childbirth should be a painful process.

Self- hypnosis can help by preparing and assisting women and their partners in pregnancy and childbirth to eliminate or reduce the need for chemical pain relief and sedation and to also reduce anxiety, worry and relaxing them. This field is receiving more and more interest both in the public and professional domains.

The aim is of self-hypnosis is to;

- Assist the woman's understanding of the child birth process
- Reduce fear and anxiety surrounding birth
- Work through any previous unpleasant birth experiences for the woman and partner
- Induce states of calm and relaxation at all stages of pregnancy and labour
- Give control back to the mother
- Reduce the need for pain relief
- Assist the mother to accept intervention should it be needed

Self-help tips for pregnancy and childbirth

- Information is one of the best ways to alleviate people's fears and child birth is no exception. Find out about the different stages of your baby's growth, the trimesters in pregnancy, labour and postpartum.

- Join a pregnancy class where you can meet other expectant mothers. These classes will help you feel prepared, be able to talk about your feelings and fears with other women in your situation, make you feel confident and in control and will also be good for socialising as pregnancy can be isolating for women when they take their maternity leave and find themselves lonely at home.

- Breathing exercises are crucial to help you calm your mind and relax so find the time to practice, they will also help a great deal during labour. (Chapter Two)

- Try and be positive- most births are straightforward and trust your body to know what to do, birthing is instinctive and believe in yourself that you can do it.

- Accepting pain- as a signalling mechanism that demonstrates the point of labour you are at, identifying with pain helps keep you informed of what stage of labour you are in, however with each person having a different pain threshold this is not always a useful technique. Pain as an avoidable part of birth that has to be tolerated and learned from- this can be seen as a challenge to the woman's coping strategies and ability to cope with varying degrees of pain ' a test of womanhood'

- Using hypnosis to assist in pregnancy and child birth works by helping you relieve anxiety, preparing your body for pregnancy and childbirth, allaying fears and dispelling myths and building trust between your mind, body and those that will be there with you at birth. The pregnancy and childbirth self-hypnosis script should be used at least late in the pregnancy (six to four weeks before the due date).

-

CHILD BIRTH SCRIPT

I will make myself as comfortable as I can ...... take a nice deep breath .... close my eyes and begin to relax ...... and think about relaxing every muscle in my body from the top of my head to the tips of my toes ...... focussing all attention on my breathing .... I will let myself breath easily and comfortably .... taking in a few slow deep breaths .... and exhaling out slowly ...... loosening any tight muscles in my body ...... as I exhale all the tightness and tension is released ...... with each breath I relax more and more ...... I let my body sink deeper and deeper into a peaceful state .... as I enter that peaceful state I continue to take deep breaths in through my nose...... and slowly letting them out my mouth ...... I let go of all the tension and thoughts ...... I observe the thoughts and let them go as they come .... I notice that my awareness of everything around me is decreasing ..... and fading away .....I am drifting into a deeper and deeper relaxation .... floating higher and higher ....

Now that I am completely relaxed .... I will imagine myself in my special place ...... I feel a sense of peace and calm in this place .... I can see it and feel it .... its peaceful and calm .... now that I am at peace and deeply relaxed my mind is completely open to all suggestions .... I will trust my mind .... because it always knows what I need .... as I am even more relaxed my eyelids become soft and heavy ...... with each breath my eyelids drift lazily down ..... softly closing as I relax deeper .... my eyes are so heavy now that I can't even open them if I try ...... I feel relaxed .... my back is relaxed .... and my baby is calm and relaxed .... I now let myself float and drift into a comfortable state of relaxation ...... I feel so much love for my baby .... I think about how much I want my baby .... and how much I love my baby .... now I am imagining directing all this love to my baby .... I imagine my baby smiling back to me .... and that my baby feels my love too ......

Now as I continue to relax I imagine the birth day arriving .... I feel the first hints of labour ...... and it is easy for me to use the breathing techniques and controlling my muscles .... I am calm and relaxed ...... breathing correctly ...... and whenever I feel discomfort I take my thoughts to my special place .... as I associate my special place with peace and calm ...... I breath slowly

.... I know exactly what to do .... whenever I feel discomfort I know what I need to do .... Now I imagine giving birth .... pushing when I need to ......breathing properly .... and feeling comfortable .... my mind is far away in my special place .... I experience the birth process ...... I push and breath .... and I feel comfortable .... because I am in control .... I am in charge of the process .... and I trust my body ......because my body knows what to do .... and what is best and safe for me ....

My delivery is successful in every way .... in every way possible .... as I imagined it ......and when my baby arrives it is healthy and strong .... healthy and strong ...... I am overjoyed .... very proud of myself .... proud of my achievement .... proud of my baby ...... now I imagine myself at home with my baby .... I am a natural mother .... just as I felt I would be .... I know instinctively how to care for my baby .... I am enjoying motherhood .... I accept the changes in my life with enthusiasm .... I see difficulties as challenges .... and I am able to meet my needs .... my baby's needs .... as well as my family's needs ..... I feel tremendous joy inside .... I am smiling ...... feeling good about myself .... and I see myself as attractive, desirable and loving ....

I will continue to enjoy my special place for another moment ...... experience it ..... drift and float .... higher and higher into a deep relaxation ...... I am feeling calm and relaxed.

When it's time to come back to full awareness .... I will count from one to five ...... and as I count from one to five .... you will begin to come back to consciousness ......

1 .... I feel myself slowly coming up from my deep relaxation
2 .... I am able to recall the room I'm in
3 .... Feeling so relaxed and peaceful
4 .... I am aware of my whole body now
5 ....I open my eyes alert, relaxed and refreshed

PREGNANCY AND CHILBIRTH AFFIRMATIONS

- I am excited to give birth to my baby
- I trust in my ability to birth my baby
- During labour and birth I am completely relaxed
- I visualise an easy, peaceful, joyous and pleasurable birth
- I am deserving of an easy uncomplicated birth
- I visualise my baby moving gently through the birth canal
- My baby is happy and healthy
- I am in control of my body
- My body is completely relaxed
- Everything is going perfectly in pregnancy
- I am in complete control of what is going on around me
- I follow my instincts and give birth in the way I desire
- I am ready and prepared for my birthing experience
- I deserve this wonderful birth
- I love my baby, my baby loves me
- I am a good mother
- I am a strong woman
- I trust my body
- My baby feels my love
- I feel my baby's love
- My body knows how to give birth
- Contractions help to bring my baby
- My pregnant body is beautiful
- My baby senses the peace I feel
- I accept my labour and birth
- I am in control of my labour
- My mind and body feel relaxed
- I will have a strong and healthy baby
- My pelvis relaxes and opens effortlessly
- My baby knows all is well
- I embrace the concept of healthy pain
- My baby knows how and when to be born
- Birth is a safe and wonderful experience
- My baby will be born strong and healthy
-

....

Chapter Twelve
Insomnia

Insomnia is difficulty getting to sleep or the ability to sleep as long as desired. It is thought that a third of people in the United Kingdom have episodes of insomnia. It tends to be more common in women and more likely to occur with age. Insomnia varies in how long it lasts and how often it occurs, it can last a short time or a long time, it can also come and go and anyone can suffer from insomnia although its more common in women who are going through the menopause, the elderly, smokers, alcoholic, and drug users.

A person's age, lifestyle, environment and diet all play a part in influencing the amount of sleep they need. Sleep is essential to human beings to be able to function properly. At least seven to eight hours of sleep are required for a healthy mind and body. As well as being unhealthy lack of sleep can be very depressing, frustrating and exhausting.

The most common symptoms of insomnia are;

- Difficulty falling asleep
- Waking up during the night
- Feeling irritable and tired and finding it hard to function during the day
- Tiredness
- Difficulty concentrating
- Headaches

Causes of insomnia

Insomnia can be caused by many different things among them are, stressful events, underlying physical conditions, psychiatric problems, alcohol and drugs use. It can also be a side effect of certain medications.

Stressful events: Some people experience insomnia due to stressful experiences for example divorce, bereavement, illness (themselves or loved ones) work problems, loss of job, money- debt problems, moving house, marriage, new baby or even a noisy neighbourhood or light and so forth.

Psychiatric problems: Underlying mental health problems can affect a person's sleep for instance;

- Mood disorders like depression or bipolar disorders.
- Anxiety disorders such as anxiety, panic attacks or post-traumatic stress disorder
- Psychotic disorders such as schizophrenia

Physical conditions: Insomnia can be caused by underlying physical conditions including

- Heart disease
- Respiratory disease like chronic obstructive pulmonary disease or asthma
- Neurological disease such as Alzheimer's or Parkinson's disease
- Hormone problems such as over active thyroids, menopause
- Joint or muscle problems like arthritis
- Problems with genital or urinary organs such as urinary incontinence or an enlarged prostate.
- Sleep disorders like restless legs syndrome, narcolepsy or sleep apnoea
- Chronic (long term) pain

Alcohol, drug and substance misuse: All these affect sleeping patterns.

Medications: Some prescribed medicines or those available over the counter can also cause insomnia for instance anti depressants, epilepsy medicine, high blood pressure, (hypertension) medicine, hormone replacement therapy(HRT) non-steroidal anti-inflammatory drugs (NSAIDS, stimulant drugs such as methylphenidate which often used to treat attention deficit hyperactivity disorder (ADHD).

The first step to treating insomnia is to find out whether the problem is being caused by an underlying medical condition. If it is then once the condition has been treated your insomnia may disappear without the need for further help. Your doctor should advise you on what you can do at home to help you sleep. The good sleep hygiene should include;

- Trying to relax before going to bed
- Avoiding napping during the day
- Establishing fixed times for going to bed and waking up
- Avoid eating heavy meals late at night
- Maintaining a comfortable sleeping environment
- Avoiding caffeine, nicotine and alcohol late at night
- Exercise within hours of bed time
- Using the bedroom mainly for sleep

Self-help tips for insomnia

- Make changes in your lifestyle for instance exercise regularly and eat a healthy balanced diet, avoid stimulants before you go to bed such as caffeine, alcohol and nicotine. Having a cup of milk or chamomile tea will aid your sleep.
- Create a comfortable sleeping environment in your bedroom and remove any distractions like television, radio and computers make sure you don't take your work into your bedroom!
- Practice meditation as research shows that meditation can have positive benefits on sleep in as little as eight weeks of practice.
- Practice relaxation techniques to calm and relax your mind before you go to bed doing so will aid easy sleep. (Chapter Two)
- Try not to sleep during the day and reserve sleep for the night.
- Avoid eating large meals in the evening.

Self-hypnosis for insomnia helps to reduce tension or minimise intrusive thoughts that may be inter-fearing with sleep. Self - hypnosis is often an effective treatment for sleep problems, it will help you relax both mentally and physically using relaxation techniques, it can also help you to understand some of the causes of insomnia.

INSOMNIA SCRIPT

I will make myself as comfortable as I can .... take a nice deep breath .... close my eyes and begin to relax ...... and think about relaxing every muscle in my body .... from the top of my head to the tips of my toes .... as I begin to focus attention on my breathing ...... my awareness of everything around me will decrease ...... I will let all the muscles in my face relax ..... around my eyes ..... and as I concentrate on relaxing this area every muscle in my body will relax ......I am drifting into a deeper and deeper level of relaxation ...... I am feeling lighter and lighter ..... floating higher and higher into a deeper level of relaxation ....I am now completely relaxed .... more relaxed than I have ever felt before .... as I experience this beautiful feeling of peace and calm .... I let go of my mind .... drift, relax and drift ......

Now that I am more deeply relaxed than ever before .... I am imagining myself in my special place .... this is a very special place for me ..... and feel my body relax ...... deeper and deeper...... as I continue to enjoy these positive feelings ..... I am are feeling lighter and lighter..........floating higher and higher into a comfortable relaxation .... my mind is at peace ...... and my body is completely relaxed ...... resting, drifting and floating into a sound and restful sleep .... from now on each night ..... night after night I will prepare to go to bed feeling calm .... and prepared for sleep to emerge .... and I will be able to feel completely relaxed ...... and at ease ...... feeling calm and relaxed .... knowing that everyday is another day complete .... and knowing tomorrow will be another opportunity to experience new challenges .... From now on .... as I move forward from this point ....as I prepare to go to sleep every night .... I will be calm .... be more and more calm ....each and every night .... feeling at ease ..... more and more at ease .... my mind and body will be released .... relaxed ..... and rested .... I will be able to sleep with tranquillity .... confidence ...... deeply ..... securely .... free and at peace .... I will sleep the best I have ever slept .... sleep as I slept as a small child .... as a baby ...... undisturbed .... settled deep .... totally immersed in a deep relaxed sleep ..... able to use all the usual noises of nature to

73

deeply sooth my sleep ...... totally at peace ...... From now on I will sleep soundly .... so soundly that I will allow my imagination and creativity to offer a deep and peaceful sleep .... a deep and restful calmness .... completely at peace .... From now on...... I will be aware of how comfortable I sleep .... as I drift deeper and deeper into a deep sleep I will become less and less aware of all the normal sounds of my surroundings ....and as I drift deeper and deeper If I experience any negative thoughts .... or worry trying to surface in my mind .... trying to disrupt my sleep ...... interfere with my rest .... I will simply sweep those thoughts away .... and replace them with positive ones .... and those positive thoughts fill my mind up as I continue to drift deeper and deeper .... my breathing is so relaxed ...... my thoughts begin to wind down .... they wind down .... and relax ...... I drift into a sound and restful sleep .... undisturbed throughout the night ...... I will awake in the morning from a deep, restful, relaxed, calm sleep ...... feeling rested and refreshed .... feeling satisfied from my deep sleep ...... and totally energised .... ready to take on the challenges of the day ..... From now on I will begin my day feeling energised ....and excited about the new opportunities the day has to offer ...... this increasing feeling of energy will begin as soon as I wake up ..... feeling inspired ...... and immersed in joy ....Because of this I will wake with an overwhelming eagerness to get up from my bed .... and into the new waiting day .... I will want to experience the day as soon as it begins .... feeling so vibrant .... enthusiastic ..... organised .... focussed .... in control .... happier with every waking moment ...... as my day evolves I will continue to maintain this inner feeling of contentment ...... satisfaction .... calmness .... alertness ...... and increasing my sense of vibrancy ...... creativity ...... resilience and energised ...... as I wake in the morning I will feel so good .... with energy running through my plans of the day ...... ready and prepared to enjoy the new day ahead ....

Everyday I will feel more healthy and alert ...... because I will have slept soundly .... deeply at peace ...... I will find more and more joy in my life .... I will continue to grow more and more in contentment .... and in my understanding of what I need to do

.... to immerse myself in effective sleep and rest patterns .... This will happen ..... from now on I will establish good night time routines ...... I will treat my bedroom with respect .... and associate it with resting and sleeping .... every time I enter my bedroom my mind will think resting and sleeping .... my bedroom will be my sanctuary .... my haven .... a place of tranquillity .... totally peaceful .... From now on when I prepare to go to sleep I will feel ready to sleep because I will go to bed with a feeling of calmness and preparedness for sleep .... every night I will go to bed ready to have a deep sleep ..... knowing that my skills of self-hypnosis will help me to feel calm and I will enjoy that deep sleep ....I will continue to enjoy my special place which is so peaceful and relaxing .... and when I am ready to come back to full awareness ...... I will count from one to five and I will come back feeling relaxed .... and with the count of five I will come back feeling calm and relaxed..

1 .... Beginning to come back
2 .... Feeling relaxed
3 .... I am aware of my normal surroundings now
4............. I am beginning to open my eyes
5 .... I open my eyes and come back feeling wonderful

INSOMNIA AFFIRMATIONS

- I am sleepy
- I fall asleep easily
- I am relaxing in my mind
- I am letting go of stress
- My body is relaxed and ready for sleep
- I am free from worrying about insomnia
- I am drifting off to sleep
- I will break free from insomnia
- I will naturally fall asleep
- I will sleep right through the night
- My sleep pattern is becoming healthier
- My body relaxes easily at the end of the day
- I have a healthy sleeping pattern

- I wake up feeling refreshed
- It feels wonderful waking up
- I am in control of my sleeping pattern
- I sleep all through the night and I will continue to do so
- I get up as soon as my alarm clock goes off feeling fresh and alert
- I feel fresh and alert when I wake up in the morning
- I enjoy a deep refreshing sleep every night
- I enjoy my sleep
- My bedroom is a place of comfort, relaxation and deep sleep
- Insomnia is no longer part of me
- When I enter my bedroom my thoughts naturally detach and slow down
- My bedroom is a place of sleep and relaxation
- I let go of my sleeping problems
- I always drift off easily to sleep
- I am always calm and relaxed at bed time, ready to drift into a deep sleep
- I feel very sleepy when my head hits the pillow
- I am always looking forward to bed time
- My sleeping problems are in the past
- I am insomnia free

···············

Chapter Thirteen
Addictions

Addiction refers to a strong uncontrollable need to repeatedly take substances and repetitive behaviours like sex, porn, gambling, internet to the extent that they have harmful consequences, causing pain and suffering to not only to the person addicted but also to their family and friends. The addiction starts out as pleasurable which triggers a powerful need for the user to carry out the activity so that they can recreate the pleasurable feelings again and again which in turn develops into a repetitive cycle whereby the person will start to depend on their addiction to cope with daily life so that the pattern becomes very difficult to break. People with addictions do not have control over what they are doing, using or taking. Nevertheless, drug addiction is not just about illegal drugs like heroine or cocaine it is reported that more than a million people in the United Kingdom are addicted to prescription drugs. Medicines can be effective if used properly but some can be addictive and dangerous if abused, drug abuse is taking a medication in a way different from what the doctor prescribed.

Common addictions
Drugs; marijuana, heroine, cocaine, inhalants, hallucinogens
- Medications- prescription drugs are the most commonly abused category of drugs behind alcohol, marijuana, cocaine and heroin, pain killers, tranquillizers, sedatives, stimulants, anti depressants, opiates, antihistamines are very addictive.
- Alcohol
- Smoking
- Sex
- Gambling
- Porn
- Food
- Internet

Difference between addiction and a habit

Addiction: With addiction a person is unable to control their addiction without help because of the mental and or physical aspects involved.

Habit: A habit is done by choice, where a person can choose to stop if they want to.

Causes of addiction

1. Genetic or family history- There is a genetic link to addiction whereby if your parents or any other family members have had addiction problems you have a higher risk of developing an addiction. Numerous studies have shown that children who have parents with addictions are more likely to develop an addiction themselves.

2. Mental health issue- Addictions tend to be more common among people who have   mental health problems for example anxiety, depression and stress.

3. Childhood appearances- Traumatic childhood experiences for example sexual abuse, emotional abuse and physical abuse can trigger addiction whereby a person is seeking for an escape from their trauma and pain from their past troubles. Because addictive feelings are pleasurable and liberating, they want to repeat it again and again as an escape route.

4. Social environment and peer pleasure- People are more at risk to addiction if they live, work, have friends, or go to school in an environment where addictive substances are used.

5. Stress – When people are stressed, they may turn to substance use to release their stress or help them cope with whatever situations they are going through. Low-self-esteem, lack of confidence, financial difficulties race, gender, sexuality, disability, poverty, homelessness, divorce, grieving, loss of parents, lack of a social life , not doing well in school can all contribute to causing stress and addiction.

Types of addictions

Physical addiction: This is where the body becomes dependent on a substance or activity so that the body cannot function without it. Physical addiction causes withdrawal effects such as vomiting, trembling, nausea, headaches. It's the body's way of telling the user that it needs to return to normal or its original state, the pain of withdrawing is often so painful that an addicted person will take another dose to ease it as soon as they can. However, although physical addiction can lead to painful and dangerous withdrawals, it's often easier to treat through detoxification.

Psychological addiction: The addiction is all in the mind- this is when the user thinks that they need the drug or activity and cannot survive without it, their whole life revolves around getting the next fix, hit or high. So psychological addiction is more or less perceived as a need. Often people fall into addiction as a result of overwhelming psychological issues for instance their addiction fulfils their needs and helps to block out negative experiences and relieve anxiety, depression and stress associated with them.

Psychological addiction is more difficult to treat than physical addiction while the body can be treated and helped to reduce desire by detoxification. Detoxification cannot cure the mind's desire. So this is where hypnosis, positive affirmations, other therapies and rehabilitation programmes step in.

Signs and symptoms of addictions

- The person takes the substance and are unable to stop themselves however much they try to.
- Withdrawal symptoms for example cravings, mood swings, bad temper, poor focus, anger, frustration, desperation, bitterness, resentment, emptiness, sweating, trembling and agitation among others.
- Increased or decreased appetite.
- Lack of sleep is also a very common withdrawal symptom.
- Addiction continues despite health problem warnings and awareness, the person continues regardless of the consequences.

- Denial is another sign of addiction as the person is not aware that he or she has a problem, they think that they are in control and can stop any time they want to which is not very easy.
- Losing interest in social activities, job, friends, family, hobbies focussing on their addiction to a point of obsession.
- Weight loss or gain due to increased or decreased appetite.
- Unexpected persistent coughs
- Pupils of eyes seeming smaller or larger than normal in drug users.
- Secretiveness
- Financial difficulties as most of or all their money is spent on the addiction.
- Changes in friendships
- Keeping stashes of drugs
- Stealing or prostitution to feed the habit
- Repetitive relapsing

Beneath everything that makes up the wiring of the human brain lies the force and intelligence that makes our minds work. Our mind plays a powerful role in causing and curing our addictions. Hypnosis is a very effective way to combat all types of addictions, it aims to get to the root of the addiction by inducing a state of heightened awareness, and in this relaxed state you become more susceptible to suggestion. Self-hypnosis will then help you gain control over your addiction while altering your ingrained behavioural patterns.

Self-help tips for addiction management

- Get to the root of the problem that is causing you the stress and addiction, find ways of dealing with it. Pushing it under the carpet will only make things worse, seek help if you feel the problem is too big for you to handle.
- Join a self-help group for addiction- support groups can be a valuable source of guidance, assistance and encouragement and you will be able to talk to other people who know how you feel and what you're going through which will help reduce fear, isolation and also help you abstain from using and staying motivated.

- Make changes in your lifestyle starting with the company you keep. If you feel that the people you're socialising with are fuelling your addiction then stop seeing them and make new friends. If you have plenty of free time on your hands do the things that you enjoy to fill that time, join a fitness club, volunteer, keep yourself busy.
- Relaxation techniques if learned and practiced will help keep your mind calm.
- Keep a positive mind and outlook on life, feel and think good about yourself.
- Don't forget you are not alone your doctor is always there for you when you feel overwhelmed and can't cope.
-

ADDICTION SCRIPT

I will make myself as comfortable as I can ...... take a nice deep breath ...... close my eyes and begin to relax ..... just thinking about relaxing every muscle in my body ...... as I begin to focus attention on my breathing .....my awareness of everything around me will decrease ..... as I feel all the tension drain from my head ...... I begin to drift into a state of deeper and deeper relaxation ..... I enjoy this pleasant feeling while my mind slowly unwinds ...... I feel comfortable, warm and relaxed ...... Now I think about the muscles in my face, jaw and neck ...... allowing this warm wave of relaxation to fill all these muscles and relax them ...... enabling them to feel comfortable and relaxed ...... I am feeling the waves of relaxation pass from my neck into my shoulders and enjoying this warm feeling as I drift into a deeper and deeper level of relaxation ...... the feeling of relaxation passes down through my shoulders to my arms reaching down to the tips of my fingers ...... my arms are now feeling tired and heavy as I sink into a deeper and deeper state of relaxation .... now my chest muscles are relaxed too and my stomach muscles ...... I focus on the gentle rise and fall of my stomach muscles as I slowly breath in and out .... now this warm relaxed feeling flows through my legs as I notice how relaxed my limbs have become ...... my mind has become totally still and deeply, deeply relaxed ...... I concentrate on how my body feels while I enjoy this deep state of relaxation .... I am feeling lighter and lighter ...... floating higher and higher into a deeper level of relaxation ...... I am now completely relaxed .... more relaxed than I have ever felt before ...... as I experience this beautiful feeling of peace and calm ...... I will just let go of my mind ...... drift, relax and drift ....

Now that I am totally, deeply relaxed and at peace with myself ...... I will imagine myself in my special place ...... this is a very special place for me ...... very peaceful and calm and filled with tranquillity ...... being in my special place makes me very calm and relaxed ..... now that I am deeply relaxed and calm .... I think about my addiction and the pain, anxiety, unhappiness, anger, confusion and how scared its made me feel ...... and now with eagerness and excitement I think about stopping my habit ...... my addiction ...... and I feel great about it ..... absolutely fine because there is no reason why I cannot stop it ..... I have a lot to gain if I end my addiction ...... and a lot to lose if I don't end my addiction ...... this is why I am making the decision to walk away free from it ...... free from the illusions that have made me think that my addiction gave me pleasure ...... and that I couldn't live without the fix my addiction gave me ...... the pleasure which didn't serve me any good purpose ......I have every reason to stop it and enjoy my life fully ...... and walk free from its slavery ...... walk free from my trap of loneliness, anger, bitterness, financial problems, lies, confusion, unhappiness ...... feeling guilty, scared, unhealthy and hopeless ....

I take my power and control back in my hands and stop those unhealthy feelings .... feelings that made me feel powerless and hopeless ...... I will stay away from all the places that trigger temptation ...... I will stay away from the people that tempt me because I am a strong person and can make all the positive changes I need to make in my life ...... and now I am going to discover again the joys of being free ...... with nothing to hide or worry about .... no more lying or hiding to feed my addiction ...... I will be able to enjoy the company of family and friendships again ...... and taking part in the activities I enjoy taking part in ..... and doing all the things that I had neglected and forgot to enjoy ...... I am now happy to be free again and that feels wonderful ...... I feel a new release of life flowing through me ...... a sense of well being and tranquillity because I know this is the right thing for me to do ...... and I will be just fine because I've just made the right decision ...... an important and major decision in my life ...... of being addiction free ...... I have given up my addiction for good ...... it has no place in my life anymore ...... and I am feeling joyous that I have finally ended the misery that addiction caused me ..... I am completely free and clean of all the toxins ...... something amazing is happening in my life ...... a major positive change is taking place ..... I feel strong and in charge ...... I am free and will continue to be free and enjoy the joys of life addiction free ...... from now and on I will be able to resist all temptation to go back into my unhealthy patterns .... I break free of all my old habits .... and toxic friendships and places .... I will stay clean and focused on being clean and healthy ...... because I know I have all the power to stop any tempting negative thoughts ...... I have the power to stay on the right path ...... and that's the only path I choose from now on ...... and that feels wonderful ..... I am free at last ...... and I will remain free ......I will enjoy my special place for another moment ...... and enjoy these positive feelings ...... drift, float and relax ...... and when I am ready to come back to full awareness .... I will count from one to ten .... and as I count from one to ten ...... I will begin to come back to full awareness ...... and I will come back feeling refreshed and relaxed

1...................Beginning to come back
2...................The background noises are coming back
3 ....Feeling relaxed
4...................I am aware of my body
5 ....Calm and peaceful
6 ....I am almost fully alert now
7 ....Feeling relaxed
8 ....I am aware of my normal surroundings
9 ....Beginning to open my eyes now
10 ....I open my eyes and come back feeling relaxed

ADDICTION AFFIRMATIONS

- I let go of old programs that keep me stuck in old habits
- I release all resistance to change
- I give myself permission to move on
- I let go of my destructive past
- I release all bad energy and toxins from my body
- I am free of my old habits
- I am worthy of love
- I treat my body with respect
- I am in control of what I put into my body
- I take back my control and power
- I am in charge of my actions
- I nourish my body and mind every day
- I trust myself and my choices
- I am good enough just as I am
- I am willing to change and take control
- What I do makes a difference
- I am a unique and special human being
- I love myself and I am surrounded by love
- Self-abuse has no place in my life
- I am growing stronger every day
- I am willing to let go of my past
- I am ready for what the future holds for me
- I am at peace with myself
- I forgive myself and everyone
- I accept all parts of myself
- I am perfect as I am a true picture of health
- My body and mind are healing and renewed
- I release all criticism of myself
- I am a worthy and perfect human being
- I claim all my power back
- My future is positive and bright
- I release all fear and doubts
- I am in a process of positive change
- I am free to move into a new chapter
- My body is healthy, whole and complete

- I trust the process of life and all is well
- I am healing and at peace with myself
- I love being me, I am perfect as I am
- Staying healthy and clean comes naturally to me
- I take back my power, I release my old ideas and destructive behaviour
- No object or person has power over me. Nothing has power over me. I am in control.
- All my addictions have left me and are no longer part of me
- All past desires mean nothing to me now I am free
- I choose to be safe and care for myself
- I am free

****

Chapter Fourteen
Lack of Confidence/Self-Esteem

Self-esteem is confidence in one's own worth and abilities and how we value ourselves based on past experiences and how others perceive us. People with more negative past experiences are more likely to have low self-esteem than the other way around.

Confidence is the belief that one can have faith in or rely on someone or something, a positive feeling arising from an appreciation of one's abilities and self-assurance.

Confidence has other meanings but it's the one above that is of interest to us. Self confidence can be very restrictive in a person's day to day life. The self doubt and negative talk of the things that you tell yourself you're not able to do, or not good enough, or deserving leads to a feeling of lack of confidence in yourself.

Once the emotional cause of why you are feeling so low has been released from your mind, that inner critic becomes quiet and you can begin to live a more confident self-assured life.

Self-hypnosis for lack of self-confidence or self-esteem will address what is causing low self-confidence and can give very rewarding results. You can find the will to fight for yourself and resolve to give yourself a shot at sorting it out and living the life you deserve.

Signs of low self-confidence/ esteem are;

- Avoiding people and situations because of fear you won't be able to cope
- Withdrawing from other people in certain situations
- Speaking quietly or mumbling or too loud to appear confident
- Anxiety, fatigue, insomnia, headaches
- Depression
- Extreme shyness
- Comfort eating
- Regular negative thinking
- Using alcohol, drugs, smoking to make a person feel more confident

- Neglect and self-abuse
- Trying to please others
- Becoming defensive when you feel judged of criticized

Common causes of low self-esteem/confidence
- Marriage breakdown and feeling like a failure
- Judgemental and critical parents
- Abuse, neglect and punishments
- Excessive criticism from teachers, sibling, peers
- Physical appearance
- Peer pressure and bullying
- Financial difficulties
- Unemployment
- Ill-health
- Addiction
- Cultural differences and feelings of not belonging
- Negative experiences

Self-help for dealing with lack of confidence
Avoid negative situations whenever possible and negative people that put you down and make you feel worthless.

- Use a journal to record positive things around you
- Whenever a negative thought creeps in , stop it right in its track and replace it with a positive one.
- Exercise regularly because when you exercise the body releases endorphins that are responsible for that "feel good factor" you get after a workout or a walk, it also keeps you fit and helps release negative toxins from the body.
- Join an activity that you enjoy doing that will help you gain confidence.
- Adopt a health life style which includes getting enough sleep, eating a balanced diet and drinking plenty of water.
- Look after yourself and do things that make you happy, a change of style, clothing, hair, new hobbies would be a good starting point!
- Stand tall, walk confidently and accept compliments

- Join a self-help group or talk to a therapist
- Put your self first always, accept and love yourself for who you are, remember you are a unique and a worthy human being.
- Seek professional help when things seem beyond your reach.

LACK OF SELF-CONFIDENCE/ SELF-ESTEEM SCRIPT

I will begin by focussing on my breath .... going deeply within .... and relaxing more and more with each breath ..... I will let myself go deeper and deeper .... into a beautiful, calm and relaxed state, deeper and deeper within .... focussing on my breathing .... as I do this I will relax my muscles ..... and feel myself going even deeper .... relaxing my facial muscles and jaw .... as a lot of tension is stored in this area .... I will then relax all the muscles of my neck .... this area stores a great deal of anxiety and tension ...... I will relax these muscles completely ...... and now I relax the muscles of my shoulders ...... letting them feel light and loose .... completely relaxed ...... I relax the muscles of my arms and my back both the lower back and the upper back .... completely relaxing them .... I relax the muscles of my stomach so that my breathing stays beautifully relaxed ...... deep .... and deep ...... and lastly, I relax ....the muscles of my legs .... completely relaxing my whole body now .... unwinding .... going deeper .... relaxing completely ..... I feel myself going even deeper .... focusing on my breathing ..... letting other noises or distractions only deepen my level of relaxation ...... even more as they fade away ....

Now that I am completely relaxed .... I imagine myself in my special place .... my mind is relaxed and I feel very calm and at peace here ...... drifting and floating with a deep sense of relaxation flowing through my entire body .... relaxing me all over .... and because I am so relaxed, I can imagine myself reaching my goal of strengthening my self-confidence and self-esteem again ...... and as my body relaxes so does my mind .... and because of this I am more receptive to all the suggestions .... everything useful that I put into my mind will become embedded there and work with me into the future ...... causing a lasting and positive impression ....

as time goes by, the things that I tell my subconscious will be a greater and greater influence on me .... the way I behave and the thoughts behind my actions ...... this effect will be lasting .... the things I accept here will go with me having a positive effect in everything I do .... as my powerful subconscious mind accepts these suggestions they will become part of me .... naturally and positively a part of me ....

As I am enjoying this relaxed and calm state and are feeling deeply relaxed ..... I feel assured that all the positive things I learn will happen to me ...... they will happen to me because they are for my own good ...... I will experience all these positive things ...... yet I will always be in control of everything .... because these suggestions are so beneficial to me and positive they will continue to happen way into the future ...... just as strongly ...... just as strongly ...... and more powerful ..... from now and onwards ...... From now on I will start to feel more and more full of energy ...... I will feel stronger, brighter and full of life ...... from now on I will open myself to the world ...... to new experiences and lose the constant thoughts about myself the way I act and concentrate totally on the things I am participating in .... and living life confidently in the world .... because of this my mind will become clearer ..... calmer and because of this I am are free to let go of the past things that have affected my self-confidence ..... to live a much happier life in the present ..... and as a result I will be able to see things more clearly ...... calmly ..... more confidently than I have done in the past ...... I am letting go this minute of those things from the past that have affected how I behave ..... how I react ...... towards other people and feel about myself .... all the negative thoughts are starting to leave and fade away from this moment ......from this moment on I will feel so much calmer ...... my emotions will be under control, accepted and worked with .... less intense ...... and sensible ...... more and more ...... and completely relaxed in every way possible .... as I become like this I will remain like this ......

I will feel more independent and confident .... more able to stick up for myself ...... fight my corner with calmness and honesty .... I will feel myself secure in my own being .... more optimistic and stronger .... I will be able to invite people into my life because I want to not because I feel that I desperately need to ...... unnecessary anxiety has gone now .... excessive worry has gone now ...... I am very confident ...... I can depend on me....... I am so calm ...... so strong and from this moment forward I will stay .... calm ...... relaxed ..... and confident .....

I will enjoy my special place for another moment, experience it .... drift and float ...... I am feeling deeply relaxed **......** calm and relaxed ...... calm and relaxed **.....**

Soon, it's time for me to come back .... and I will come back to awareness by counting from one to ten ..... when I say ten I will open my eyes ...... I will be wake up alert and in full control of my body and mind .... feeling wonderful, refreshed, relaxed, filled with positive and beautiful energy.

One ...... two .... three .... more and more awake, feeling alert, feeling wonderful ...... five .... six .... more and more awake, feeling great .... seven .... eight .... nearly awake now .... nine .... ten .... feeling relaxed ....

LACK OF CONFIDENCE AFFIRMATIONS
Confidence flows abundantly into my life

- I naturally attract confident people to me because I am confident
- My actions exude confidence
- I act with confidence
- I love and accept myself unconditionally
- I am a well loved and well respected person
- People love me for who I am
- My self-esteem allows me to accept compliments easily and also freely compliment others
- I have high self-esteem because I respect myself and others
- Gratitude moves me towards high self-esteem and confidence

- I am in control of my emotions
- I release the need to prove myself to anyone as I am my own self and love it that way
- Being self confident suits me perfectly fine
- My self-esteem radiates from my grateful heart
- I have a high level of self-esteem
- I am confident in myself
- I make life decisions with confidence and conviction
- I am confident and strong
- I feel good inside and out
- I move confidently in the direction of my dreams
- I am perfect just the way I am
- I am in control of my life
- I am confident in everything I do
- My self-esteem is high because I honour who I am
- It is safe for me to speak for myself
- I choose to feel good about myself
- I am worthy of my own love
- I accept others as they are and in turn they accept me as I am
- I am a wonderful and unique human being and I feel great
- I have the power, confidence, and self-esteem to move forward in life with ease
- I love myself unconditionally
- I set and achieve goals easily
- I am an achiever
- I am a winner and attract success
- I can do anything I set my mind on
- Everyday I become more self-confident
- I project a positive self-esteem
- I am unique and I am confident in my uniqueness

....

Chapter Fifteen
Anger Management

Anger is a natural human emotion in response to annoyance, displeasure, irritability, threats, injustice, or hostility. Anger inspires powerful harmful feelings and behaviours which allows us to fight and defend ourselves when we face attack therefore a certain amount of anger is necessary for our survival. Anger can be expressed, suppressed or re-directed and can vary in intensity from mild to extreme. We all get angry at some point in our lives because anger is a normal healthy emotion but we experience and express anger in different ways. Even though anger is a natural human emotion, too much anger can have serious consequences to health, relationships, work, family and state of mind and can also cause harm to ourselves and other people. Anger for sure does more harm than good, causes feelings of revenge, blaming others, is very negative and creates fear and anxiety.

Anger becomes dangerous to our health when it's against our best interests and others. If you find yourself responding to many situations with anger or violence then you may have a problem and should seek help to manage your anger.

Types of anger

Passive anger: Is the type of anger when emotions are displayed as meanness or sarcasm, it's a repressed kind of anger so it can be hard to recognise.

Aggressive anger: With this anger a person is aware of their emotions but don't know the roots of their anger, such anger can lead to intense damage of possessions.

Sudden anger: Comes from nowhere, it happens quickly and is usually over as quickly as it comes although it might leave damage.

Chronic anger: This type of anger happens for no reason at all, with this form of anger a person is almost angry all the time, it's a very damaging type of anger.

Behavioural anger: Is usually aimed at whatever has triggered it, and can end in physical abuse.

Paranoid anger: feelings of jealous towards others as the person feels intimidated by them.

Verbal anger: Is mainly expressed with words, insults, criticism, and putting others down.

Volatile anger: Comes and goes in varying degrees and can be expressed verbally or physically.

Self-inflicted anger: This self harming anger, a person punishing themselves for something they have done of which they feel ashamed of and also being highly critical of themselves. Examples of self-inflicted anger are, over eating, self cutting and other self-harming habits.

Causes of anger

- Psychological disorders such as anxiety disorder, depressive disorder
- Stress
- Financial problems
- Relationship problems
- Abuse- Physical or verbal
- Medication and drugs such as sedatives, amphetamines, tranquilizers, cocaine, hypnotics, nicotine, alcohol, caffeine
- Grief
- Disappointment
- Mistreatment
- Threat- self and loved ones
- Illness
- Criticism
- Feelings of being judged

Physical symptoms of anger

- Headaches
- Fatigue
- Heart palpitations
- Increased blood pressure
- Stomach ache

- Sweating of palms
- Feeling hot in the face- redness
- Dizziness
- Shaking or trembling
- Tense muscles
- Clenched jaw

Emotional symptoms of anger
- Irritability
- Anxiety
- Sadness
- Depression
- Stress
- Guilty feelings
- Fear
- Mood swings
- Bitterness
- Resentment
- Aggression
- Panic
- Worry
- Paranoia and loss of control
-

Self-help tips for dealing with anger
1. Counting to ten- this distracts you from whatever started your anger and by doing so, you are putting your energy into and also concentrating on something else rather than your anger.
2. Try and distract yourself and do something you enjoy doing for example you can go for a walk, a jog, walk the dog, listen to calming music, chat to a friend, meditate or pray-whatever makes you feel good and by doing that, you will be channelling all your anger and negativity into something good and positive.
3. Control your voice- speak in a low tone but still in a firm manner and calmly, raising your voice will only increase your anger. Your goal in a argument should always be quality not quantity

4. If you are in the wrong say sorry and mean it however hard it is, if the other person is in the wrong accept their apology, as it's often said sorry is a very small word but unfortunately the hardest word to say but it can soften even the most hardened of hearts and incredibly brighten any situation. Moreover so many good things can come out of it!

5.Try relaxation techniques such as deep breathing which can help calm down angry feeling, whenever you feel angry breath in deeply and slowly and out as many times as you need until the anger leaves your body. (Chapter Two)

The role of anger management is to control and reduce your emotional feelings caused by anger. Self-Hypnosis in anger management can help to change the way a person thinks or reacts in situations that causes their anger explosions, by accessing the subconscious mind, self-hypnosis can often help the person learn how to deal with their anger in a positive, calm and more relaxed way.

ANGER MANAGEMENT SCRIPT

I will make myself as comfortable as I can ...... take a nice deep breath ...... close my eyes and begin to relax ..... just thinking about relaxing every muscle in my body ...... as I begin to focus attention on my breathing .....my awareness of everything around me will decrease ..... feeling all the tension drain from my head ...... I begin to drift into a state of deeper and deeper relaxation ..... I enjoy this pleasant feeling while my mind slowly unwinds ...... I feel comfortable, warm and relaxed ...... Now I think about the muscles in my neck ...... allowing this warm wave of relaxation to fill all the muscles in my neck ...... enabling my neck to feel comfortable and relaxed ...... I am feeling the waves of relaxation pass from my neck into my shoulders and enjoying this warm feeling I drift into a deeper and deeper level of relaxation ...... the feeling of relaxation passes down through my shoulders to my arms reaching down to the tips of my fingers ...... my arms are now feeling tired and heavy as I sink into a deeper and deeper state of relaxation .... now my chest muscles are relaxed too and my stomach muscles ...... I focus on the gentle rise and fall of my stomach muscles as I slowly breath in and out .... now this warm relaxed feeling flows through my legs as I notice how relaxed my limbs have become ...... my mind has become totally still and deeply, deeply relaxed ...... I concentrate on how my body feels while I enjoy this deep state of relaxation .... I am feeling lighter and lighter ...... floating higher and higher into a deeper level of relaxation ...... I am now completely relaxed .... more relaxed than I have ever felt before ...... as I experience this beautiful feeling of peace and calm ...... I will just let go of my mind...... drift, relax and drift ....

Now that I am totally deeply relaxed and at peace with myself ...... I will imagine myself in my special place ...... this is a very special place for me ...... very peaceful and calm and filled with tranquillity ...... being in my special place makes me very calm and relaxed ..... now I imagine thinking about my anger and the pain , anxiety, unhappiness, confusion and fear it has caused me and the people I love ...... and now with eagerness and excitement I think about being able to manage my anger .... and I feel great about it ..... absolutely fine because there is no reason why I cannot stop it ..... I have a lot to gain if I am able to manage my anger .... and a lot to lose if I don't sort it out ...... anger is dangerous to my health and can also cause harm to other people ...... it does more harm than good ...... this is why I am making the decision to walk away free from it ...... free from the outbursts of anger, and rage that make me an unpleasant person to be around ...... my anger doesn't serve me any good purpose ...... only bad comes out of it and therefore I have every reason to stop it and enjoy my life fully ...... be able to walk free from its slavery ...... walk free from my anger .... from .... bitterness, revenge, blame, resentfulness, aggression, fights, confusion, unhappiness ...... feelings of guilt and hopelessness .... I take my power and control back in my hands and stop these unhealthy feelings .... feelings that make me feel powerless, hopeless and a bad person ...... I know I am a strong person and can make all the positive changes I need to make in my life ...... managing my anger .... and now I am going to discover again the joys of being anger free ...... with nothing to be anxious or worry about .... no more fighting with my family, friends, workmates ...... its okay to be angry but not act out of emotion ...... its okay to be angry and let myself feel whatever it is I am angry about but not reacting .... when I am angry I will breathe in and out slowly and turn my attention to my feelings ...... or I will count from one to ten and feel the anger go through me and out of me as it leaves my body .... leaving me feeling calm and relaxed ...... without reacting at all ...... anger is an emotion so it comes and goes and doesn't stay for ever therefore very easy to control .... I will always be able to control my anger without reacting at all ...... I have chosen to deal with it by simply breathing in and out slowly as long as I need to or count from one to ten until all the anger has left my body .... these are my new ways of dealing with my anger the healthy way .... and I am just .... because they work for me ..... when I am angry I will always keep my voice down and not raise it .... I will always say sorry if I am in the wrong or accept an apology if I'm given one .... and that's fine with me .... I am now happy to be free again and that feels wonderful ...... I feel a new release of life flowing through me ...... a sense of well being and positive changes taking place ......because I know this is the right thing for me to do ...... and I will be just fine because I've just made the right decision ...... an important and major decision in my life ...... of managing my anger...... I am giving up my extreme anger outbursts for good ...... anger has no place in my life anymore ...... and I am feeling joyous that I have finally ended the misery that it caused me and the people I care for ..... I am completely free and clean of all the anger toxins, rages, irritation, depression, and anxiety ...... something amazing is happening in my life ...... a major positive change is taking place ..... I feel strong and in charge ...... I feel free of the excess anger I had stored in my body ...... its all leaving me and fading away ...... with each day I am more and more calm and clear ..... I am free because I am in control of my anger now...... and will continue to be free, calm and relaxed enjoying life to the full ...... from now on I will be free ...... because I have the power to control and stop my anger and any negative thoughts that trigger it ...... I have the power to stay on the right path ...... and that's the only path I choose from now on ...... and that feels wonderful ..... I am free at last ...... and I will remain anger free ......I will enjoy my special place for another moment ...... take all those positive feelings in ...... and bring them back with me ..... drift and float ...... I am feeling calm and relaxed ...... In a few minutes I will come back to awareness ...... I will count from one to ten .... and as I count from one to ten ...... I will begin to come back to full awareness ...... I will come back feeling relaxed ....

1...................Beginning to come back
2................... The background noises are coming back
3 ....Feeling relaxed
4................... I am aware of my body
5 ....Calm and peaceful
6 ....I am almost fully alert now
7 ....Feeling relaxed
8 ....I am aware of my normal surroundings
9 ....I am beginning to open my eyes now
10 ....I open my eyes and come back feeling wonderful

ANGER MANAGEMENT AFFIRMATIONS

I have the power to manage my anger
- I am in control of my emotions
- I am in control of the way I react in stressful situations
- I am calm, focused and relaxed
- I remain calm in frustrating situations
- I am able to channel my anger into something positive
- I always speak in a calm and low voice in frustrating situations
- I am able to calm myself down by breathing in deeply
- I am always in control of myself
- I am successfully managing my anger
- Each day I become less and less angrier
- Each day I become more and more calmer
- Thinking positively in difficult situations is becoming more easy
- Managing my anger comes naturally to me
- I am breaking free from my anger

- I am a strong person unaffected by negative words
- I choose to act and think positively
- I feel good inside and out because I am anger free
- I say sorry when I am in the wrong and it makes me feel good
- I accept apologies and that's fine too and feels amazing
- I forgive freely and set myself free from the anger
- I decide to create thoughts that bring me peace and happiness
- I move forward into the future anger free
- I have a great life and I am grateful for it
- I can feel angry but stay calm and in control at the same time
- I have the power to control my reactions
- I am in total charge of my thoughts and actions
- I am perfectly managing my anger
- I feel calm and at peace with myself

....

Chapter Sixteen
Nail Biting

Nail biting is a common stress relieving habit. People bite their nails for all sorts of reasons such as anxiety, nerves, boredom, stress or excitement. It can also be a learned behaviour from family members. Sometimes people bite their nails without realising it, for example while on the phone, reading, watching television. Nail biting includes biting the cuticle and soft tissue surrounding the nail. People of all ages bite their nails;

- About half of all children between the ages of 10 and 18 bite their nails at one time or another. Nail biting is very common during puberty.
- Some young adults ages 18-22 years bite their nails
- Only a small number of other adults bite their nails. Most people stop biting their nails on their own by age 30.
- Boys bite their nails more often than girls after age 10.

Hypnosis has proven to be one of the most straightforward and effective ways of helping people stop biting their nails. During self-hypnosis you will be communicating direct to your subconscious mind which will help you to stop your behavioural pattern, mostly people are not aware when they bite their nails, self-hypnosis will make you aware and allow you to stop biting your nails.

NAIL BITING SCRIPT

I am going into a state of deep relaxation ..... slowly and surely my entire body and mind relaxing ..... relaxing ...... relaxing ..... I am going deeper and deeper and deeper into a state of deep relaxation ..... each and every muscle of my body is now relaxing ....everything is so peaceful and quiet ......One, the muscles of my face are relaxing ...... relaxing .... and relaxing ......Two, the muscles of my neck are slowly loosening .... and relaxing ......Three, the muscles of my shoulders are losing their stiffness ...... relaxing ..... relaxing

....Four, both my hands are totally free ...... and their muscles are relaxing ..... relaxing ......Five, the muscles of my stomach are relaxing .... relaxing ..... relaxing ....

And lastly, the muscles of my legs are slowly relaxing .... relaxing ..... relaxing ......Now that my body and mind are completely relaxed ...... I will begin to focus attention on my breathing ..... my awareness of everything around me will decrease ...... and all the background noises are fading away ...... relaxing me even more and more ..... deeper and deeper into a comfortable relaxation ...... I am drifting into a deeper and deeper level of relaxation ..... I feel heavy ...... like a heavy weight being lifted off my shoulders ...... I am feeling lighter and lighter .... floating higher and higher into a deeper level of relaxation.

I am now completely relaxed .... more relaxed than I have ever felt before .... as I experience this beautiful feeling of peace and calm ...... I will just let go of my mind .... drift .... relax and drift .

Now that I am deeply relaxed ...... I am imagining myself in my special place .... this is a very special place for me ..... feeling it ...... sensing it ...... and seeing it ...... feeling my body relax ..... deeper and deeper...... as I enjoy these tranquil feelings .... I am feeling lighter and lighter....... floating higher and higher into a comfortable relaxation ....I feel wonderful inside and out. This is my time ...... no one wants anything from me ...... no one needs anything ...... this time its just for me ...... and maybe now is the time for me to give myself permission to let changes take place .... my body feels free ...... lighter ...... my muscles feel released ....yet stronger .... I am feeling at peace .... deeply relaxed and ready to deal with the day more effectively .... I notice that my breathing is slower .... stable ....and deeper .... this feeling is so much better .... so much more at peace .... and as I am relaxing deeper and deeper .... I reflect for a moment on all the success I have achieved in the past .... the many positive goals that I have already reached .... and feeling proud of myself .... proud of myself ...... and because I have been successful in the past and because I have reached so many goals ..... I will continue to be successful in every area of my life ...... I am now more motivated and determined than ever before to reject my nail biting habit ....because it is unhealthy and harmful to me ...... I now reject this habit of nail biting ...... I have all the right reasons to get rid of it .... I do it for myself .... for my health and well being and that feels fine ..... it feels the right thing to do ...... my mind and body rejects nail biting .... I am Imagining having healthy well formed nails .... and that feels great ...... I have made up my mind to stop biting my nails ...... I have made the choice to be free of nail biting ...... the thought of me biting nails now is disgusting .... and the taste and texture of nails in your mouth is unappetizing .... so unhealthy ...... my mouth is clear of nails and it feels fresher than it has ever felt before .... I see myself going through my daily routine without biting my nails .... and feeling fine .... feel just fine .... as I find myself in this delightful state of relaxation I notice how my body and mind feels .... I feel more calm and in control ...... I will stay calm and say to myself ...... this is my new way of dealing with my nail biting habit .... when I say calm and stop .... I will feel more and more relaxed .... this is a successful way .... and it works ...... and I feel fine with it .... I will continue imagining myself in the future caring for my nails .... I notice how nicely they have grown ...... and how beautiful they look .... I love my new nails and I feel very good about myself ...... there is a big smile on my face .... I am no longer a nail biter ...... and my emotions are fine .... I feel just fine .... it feels fine being free of my nail biting habit .... the less I bite my nails the better I feel .... every aspect of my life will begin to improve .... more and more .... I am free of nail biting .... I no longer bite my nails ...... I see myself in the future enjoying myself ...... feeling great without biting nails ..... feeling calm .... and that feels fine ....

I will enjoy my special place for another moment, experience it ...... drift and float....... feeling calm and relaxed ......In a few minutes when I am ready to come back to awareness ...... I will count from one to ten .... and as I count from one to ten .... I will begin to come back to full awareness ...... I will come back feeling relaxed.

1.................Beginning to come back
2.................All the background noises are coming back again
3 ....I am able to recall the room I am in
4.................I am feeling calm and completely relaxed
5 ....I am aware of my whole body
6 ....Feeling calm and peaceful
7 ....I am aware of my surroundings and all the
            background noises
8 ....Feeling so calm and relaxed
9 ....Begin to open my eyes now
10 ....I come back feeling completely relaxed

NAIL BITING AFFIRMATIONS

  I am free from nail biting
- I am aware of my hands and fingers
- I am relaxed without needing to bite my nails
- My hands and fingers are relaxed
- I keep my fingers away from my mouth
- My nails are healthy and beautiful
- I take proper care of my nails rather than biting them
- I am in total control of my body
- I always clip my nails rather than bite them
- I have overcome my nail biting habit
- I am in control of my impulses
- I release my need to bite my nails
- I love myself
- I love my body
- I love my hands and fingers
- My fingers are healthy
- I am no longer a nail biter
- I feel good about myself
- I am a strong person
- I resist the urge to bite my nails easily
- Resisting biting my nails comes naturally to me
- I am free of nail biting
- I am in control of my body

- I choose not to bite my nails again
- I feel good inside and out
- I feel confident about myself with my healthy and good looking hands
- Nail biting is in my past
- I am free of nail biting

****

Chapter Seventeen
Sports Performance

Being a successful athlete involves maintaining high levels of physical fitness. However this is only part of the strategy required for success. According to research, sports performance has more to do with mental abilities than physical abilities. This may sound strange to some people but a vast number of sports people have recognised the power of their mental state having a positive effect on their sports performance and because all athletes regardless of their sport desire constant improvement to be at their best, mental development is now widely considered and included in training. Using imagery, visualization and relaxation is now a common practice in all sports as it helps improve mental strength, overcome sports injuries, improve performance, improve focus and concentration, help in overcoming mental blocks, boosting confidence and controlling emotions in both training and competition.

Hypnosis has been used for many years to help professional athletes improve their natural ability. Successful athletes are often able to control their state of mind so they have a psychological advantage which prevents them from under-performing or getting nervous.

Hypnosis helps to engage the athletes' mind in a positive way to help them focus on their goals and achieve them. Being able to control negative thoughts and emotions is the basis of sports psychology and can often be achieved through hypnosis. Sports people refer to this as being in the 'zone'. This means that they get totally absorbed in what they are doing and hardly notice what is happening when performing their best. Hypnosis helps in accessing the zone so that they can use it to enhance their performance. Hypnosis can help with most sports including golf, football, swimming, darts, running, cricket, boxing, cycling, tennis and many more.

Self-help tips for sports performance

- A healthy balanced diet will have a great effect on your ability to perform and it will get the best fitness and sports results.
- Work on your mental skills as this is equally important, visualization, imagery and relaxation.
- Hydrate before, during and after performing, dehydration will have a negative impact on your performance.
- Have plenty of rest-resting your body and mind will make you feel better going into your next training or competition.
- Plenty of training and exercising is required to perfect your skill.

SPORTS PERFORMANCE SCRIPT

I will make myself as comfortable as I can ...... take a nice deep breath, close my eyes and begin to relax .... just thinking about relaxing every muscle in my body .....from the top of my head to the tips of my toes ...... as I begin to focus attention on my breathing ...... my awareness of everything around me will decrease ..... I will relax all my muscles ...... I am becoming more and more aware of my breathing ...... as it slows down more and more ...... I inhale and exhale .... the sounds around me are unimportant I let them come and go ..... until they completely fade away ...... I release all tension and stress in my body .... I am drifting into a deeper and deeper level of relaxation ...... feeling lighter and lighter ......floating higher and higher into a deeper level of relaxation ......

As I am now completely relaxed .... more relaxed than I have ever felt before .... I will imagine myself in my special place .... a special place just for me ...... I am alone here and there is no one to demand anything from me .... its just me .... this is my time in my special place .... I can see it and feel it ...... its the most peaceful place in the world for me .... I feel a sense of peace flow through me ...... I feel positive ...... these positive feelings growing stronger and stronger .... I will remain calm, peaceful and positive no matter what's going on around me .... all the stress and pressure will bounce off and away from me .... and these positive feelings will stay with me and grow stronger and stronger with each day and onwards .... I am drifting and relaxing deeper and deeper

106

.... I feel wonderful inside and out .... Now I that I am deeply relaxed ...... I will imagine a day .... a perfect day when I wake up and everything just feels right ...... and I think about today and how it is the most important race of my life .... today is the day that I am going to show every one especially myself ..... what I can do .... what I am capable of ...... today is the day when I have absolute certainty ...... and I feel it in every heartbeat .... I can feel it in my mind .... as I think about it I can feel a wave of relaxation spreading all throughout my body from the top of my head to the tips of my toes .... I feel relaxation going through my body .... totally relaxed .... and that is the relaxation feeling I get when I perform ...... I imagine myself engaging in my sport .... as I perform ...... competing with others ...... I am very good as an individual player as well as a team player ...... I enjoy my sport .... I am confident and strong .... and my attitude towards my opponents is good ...... now I imagine myself getting ready for my competition .... my mind wanders off .... I see the track ...... the field .... the pool .... the people .... the officials .... my opponents .... the time keepers .... none of that is important .... none of that bothers me ..... because I am here to win .... before I start I take a nice deep breath .... and relax my entire body .... focussing the attention on what I am going to do .... and my movements .... I am able to keep my concentration for as long as I want ..... everything is prepared ...... and I am fit and strong ..... and all the training I had ...... all that preparation ...... is coming back to me .... is about to pay off .... I feel totally composed ...... completely at ease and relaxed ...... ready for what is to come .... everything around me goes quiet .... I am looking straight ahead .... visualising every move I am about to take .... visualising my win .... the shutter goes off and I see myself act and react .... moving perfectly ..... with every muscle in harmony with my thoughts ...... I see my strategy going to plan ...... and feeling lighter and relaxed .... strong and relaxed ...... alert and clear minded .... In the back of my head there is a voice saying "This is easy", " I have done it ", " I have won " .... this is how it should be and I feel fulfilled .... complete ...... happy ...... my legs are moving swiftly ..... my arms are working perfectly ...... and all that training comes in automatically .... and suddenly I become aware that people are cheering ...... applauding .... willing on me .... the people watching .... the people in my mind ...... and I don't think about it because I am determined and focussed on winning .... powering right to the end .... and now I see myself win .... I feel pleased with myself ...... proud of myself ...... I feel great ...... about every correct move .... every bit of my performance .... my winning .... is all imprinted into my subconscious mind so that I can repeat my perfect game over and over like a film ...... and see it in great detail .... imagining myself making all the right moves and putting on the best performance of my life ...... and winning .... still in my deeply relaxed state I will continue to enjoy my special place .... allowing myself to feel my body making the changes ...... adjustments ...... learning .... until I am ready to come back to the present .... and when I am ready to come back to awareness I will count from one to five .... in my mind .... and when I get to five ...... I will be back in the present .... feeling refreshed positive and relaxed ....

1 .... I am beginning to come back
2 .... I am feeling calm and relaxed
3........ My awareness of my surroundings is returning
4 .... I am beginning to open my eyes
5 ...... I open my eyes and come back feeling calm and relaxed

SPORTS PERFORMANCE AFFIRMATIONS

  I am a fierce competitor
- I am dedicated to my sport
- I am dedicated to my training
- I train consistently
- I stay focussed at all times
- I am a brilliant at my sport
- I have great stamina
- I am motivated to practice
- I am a skilled sports person

I will exceed my expectations and the expectation of others
- I become better and better with each day
- I always and will always perform my best
My stamina increases with each day
- My endurance is high
- Winning is the best feeling in the world
- I am naturally a focused and dedicated person
- I work hard at my sports and my hard work is paying off
- Motivation is a big part of my life
- I am confident in my sporting ability
- I am focused on winning my games
- I am improving everyday
- I am very calm and relaxed when performing
- I am in control of my mind and body when competing
- Winning comes naturally to me
- I am proud of myself and my achievements
- I am focused, strong and relaxed when performing
- My mind is alert and clear when I am competing
- I make all the right moves and give a polished performance
- I always perform my best
- Winning is second nature to me
- I am feeling good inside and out and fit
- I always feel confident before a game
- I am motivated to win
- I am well prepared to give an outstanding performance
- My body knows what to do and how to move
- My ability and strength always shine through
- I am a born winner

****

Chapter Eighteen
Motivation

Motivation is derived from the word "Motive". Motivation is the inner power that pushes us to achieve a goal. Motivation is powered by desire and ambition. It is a process of stimulating people to act on accomplishing goals. Motivation is one of the most important keys to success and can be applied to any action or goal. Lack of it means less chance in succeeding in whatever a person sets out to do in life. Motivation instils happiness, energy and positivity. The process of motivation consists of three stages:

1- A felt need or drive
2- A stimulus in which needs have to be aroused
3- When needs are satisfied, the satisfaction or accomplishment of goals

Self-hypnosis for motivation helps with getting rid of any past negative programming, improving self-projection, increasing confidence and self-acceptance and changing your perspective on your relationship to a given problem.

Self-help tips for motivation

- Set yourself a goal this will make it easier for you to motivate yourself to move forward to where you want to be.
- Be persistent and patient, however hard work your goal is, don't give up just because you've had a setback. Success is all about grafting.
- Positive thinking will take you a long way so be positive
- Set yourself a deadline and stick with it, when you have achieved your goal reward yourself for the hard work.
- Socialise with people who inspire you and keep you motivated
- Visualization techniques will help you create a mental picture of what you what to achieve. Seeing yourself already achieving your goal makes your brain believe that attaining that goal is possible.

Focussing consistently on your goal will enable you to manifest it sooner and bring it within your grasp.

MOTIVATION SCRIPT

I will make myself as comfortable as I can ...... take a nice deep breath ...... close my eyes and begin to relax ...... just thinking about relaxing every muscle in my body ..... from the top of my head to the tips of my toes ...... as I begin to focus attention on my breathing ...... my awareness of everything around me will decrease ...... I let all the muscles in my body relax ...... from the top of my head to my toes and as I continue to do this I can feel all the tension and stress leave my mind and body .... I begin to drift into a deeper and deeper relaxation ...... I am feeling lighter and lighter ...... floating higher into an even deeper level of relaxation ..... now that I am completely relaxed ...... more relaxed than I have ever felt before ...... and as I experience this beautiful feeling of peace and calm ...... I just let go of my mind ...... drift ...... relax ....and drift .

Now I am imagining myself in my special place ...... I can feel it and see it .... this is the most peaceful place in the world for me .... here I am alone and there is no one to disturb me or ask for anything .... its just me ...... in my special place .... my special time .... I can feel a sense of peace flow through me .... and a sense of well-being .... relaxing deeper and deeper .... Because I am deeply relaxed now .... my subconscious mind will accept the new suggestions .... for my motivation and self empowerment .... I am imagining reaching my goals and becoming a successful person with nothing holding me back .... I am imagining myself pushing back the barriers I have created .... and instead I am creating opportunities and expanding my horizons .... achieving my goals ...... reaching higher and higher .... feeling comfortable and at ease with my expanded boundaries .... I feel secure and pleased that I have control and power within myself to change .... to change my limitations and be the successful person I want to be ...... I feel good ...... confident ...... at peace and content ......I am now free of past burdens ..... I am secure .... confident .... self-assured and I feel centred and strong ..... now I am imagining all the goals I want to achieve .... I see new opportunities and new challenges that are more exciting than the old ones .... I see myself with renewed energy ..... I am enthusiastic and focussed than ever before .... new ideas develop and positive feelings ...... I am reaching for my goal ......

I am successful and I am worthy of all the good things life has to offer ...... reaching my goals is very beneficial to me ...... and as I continue to reach the goals in my life ...... I see them as positive events ...... positive for me ...... positive for my family .... positive for my friends ...... and positive for the people I work with .... I reflect on all the other things I have achieved in my life .... and know that I am capable succeeding again .... in reaching my goals ...... I see myself become successful ...... I am happy and comfortable in my success .... I use my success in positive and worthwhile ways ...... I deserve to be successful ...... I can see it ...... I can feel it ......

I am successful ...... I see myself as intelligent, creative and confident ...... I have many choices and options .... and whatever direction I choose to take .... I know it will be the right one for me ...... every choice and direction I take from now on will be the absolute right one for me ...... I can see myself clearly in the future with many positive directions and choice ...... and I bring this image to the present ...... and I see myself successful .... confident and with many wonderful path ways to choose ..... and I know I will continue to be successful and continue to make choices that enhance my life ......

I will enjoy your special place for another moment ..... take all these positive feelings in ...... and bring them back with me to the present ..... drifting and floating ......I am are feeling calm and relaxed ...... In a few minutes I will come back to awareness .... I will count from one to five and as I count from one to five ......I will begin to come back to full awareness ......I will come back feeling relaxed.

1 ....Beginning to come back
2 .... The background noises are coming back
3 ....Feeling relaxed

4 .... I am beginning to open my eyes

5 .... I open my eyes and come back feeling at peace and relaxed

MOTIVATION AFFIRMATIONS

I am a highly motivated person

- I am motivated at all times
- I am always motivated and always get things done on time
- I am highly motivated, ambitious and driven
- I find it easy to motivate myself
- I have high energy drive and motivation
- My positive energy motivates me
- I am becoming more and more motivated every single day
- I find motivation when I need it
- I am getting more and more driven and ambitious
- I am hugely motivated and productive
- I am becoming more and more motivated in all areas of my life
- Each day I wake up more motivated
- Being motivated is a part of life I enjoy
- Being motivated and driven is part of who I am
- Motivation comes naturally to me
- I can do anything I set my mind on
- I can I can I can do it is my mantra
- I think of only positive things and positive things happen in my life
- I am a go getter and will not stop at anything to achieve my goals
- I am always successful, success is in my blood
- I enjoy challenges, I take them on and win over them
- Motivation comes to me from inside.
- I am my own motivator
- My goal is my motivation. I see only the goal till the time I reach it
- I know my worth. I deserve success
- Life is beautiful. Life is fulfilling. I love life.
- I always give my best and attract the best
- I am successful through motivation

•••••••••••••••

Chapter Nineteen
Fear of Flying

Fear of flying is also called aerophobia, it's a common problem which can limit a person's horizons and it's caused by the unconscious part of the mind warning you that its dangerous to get on a plane. It would be okay for that to happen if the plane is in an unfit condition to fly, however in the case of a flying phobia the protection mechanism which is meant to keep you safe has become very sensitive and is now causing a problem.

Aerophobics respond differently to fear of flying although the most common reaction is to avoid flying, which keeps the fear alive and makes the sufferer even more anxious. It is important that you accept that you have a problem and start taking steps to overcome it which will take a lot of courage and practice and also identify your triggers which are very many, it might be terrorism, fear of crashing, turbulence, take off, landing, fear of heights, being in a confined space or being far from home. If this fear is affecting and limiting your life in any way that you don't like then you should not accept it as normal.

Self-hypnosis can help the sufferer with the fear of flying psychologically and quickly by helping you to overcome your fear and becoming more confident about flying. Self- hypnosis can also help you to learn a new pattern of behaviour and relaxation skills. Many people have used it not only to overcome their fear of flying but also to look forward to flying and to enjoy it!

Causes of aerophobia

The cause of fear of flying is disputed. While most researchers believe its a learned fear, other factors may also contribute to it such as: stressful life events, personality factors, misinformation about the danger of flying, biological predisposition, worrying about the dangers of flying, fear of heights, fear of enclosed spaces, fear of crowded conditions, sitting in hot stale air, being dependent on the pilot's judgement, not being in control and the possibility of terrorism.

FEAR OF FLYING SCRIPT

I will make myself as comfortable as I can .... starting by concentrating on my breathing .... close my eyes and begin to relax every muscle in my body .... from the top of my head to the tips of my toes ...... as I concentrate on my breathing .... I am beginning to notice that the noises around me are starting to fade into the background ...... helping me to relax even more and more .... deeper and deeper......... more deeply relaxed than I have ever felt before ...... I am letting all the muscles in my body relax ...... starting with the muscles in my face .... letting them relax ...... relaxing the muscles around my eyes and my neck .... this feeling travels nicely and gently into my shoulders ...... the wave of relaxation travels on through my arms and fingers ..... and into my chest .... my breathing is deeper and slower focussing on the relaxation that my body is experiencing .... and realising just how good this feels .... now the relaxation is going down into my stomach ...... its very calm and peaceful .... and the feeling has reached my hips now .... very slowly travelling down my legs .... into the large muscles in my thighs .... and then down into my feet .... filling them with total relaxation ..... I notice that this feeling of total relaxation has filled every part of me with peace and tranquillity ..... I am now feeling deeply and completely relaxed ..... just letting my mind drift .....relax and drift .... deeper and deeper ......

Now that I am completely relaxed .... I am imagining myself in my special place .... the most relaxing and peaceful place for me .... in this place no one wants anything from me .... it's just for me .... time for myself to relax and enjoy .... in this place my body relaxes deeper and deeper .... and mind becomes calmer and calmer .... I am feeling lighter and lighter .... floating higher and higher into a comfortable relaxation .... I feel wonderful inside and out .... I am completely relaxed and because I am so relaxed .... I am imagining reaching my goal of overcoming my fear of flying .... my subconscious is completely ready to listen .... and to absorb everything .... I will let my mind drift back in time .... and as I begin to drift easily back in time .... I know that I am protected by my own positive energy .... I will continue to drift back in time and let my mind think about my fear .... the fear of flying .... my phobia that frightens me .... I will let my mind go back in time where my fear started .... knowing that here and now I am safe and secure .... going back to the first time I experienced my fear .... I can see everything at a distance ...... seeing it as a movie on the screen .... at a safe distance .... I am feeling fine and calm .... I begin to understand why I felt fearful .... as I gain more understanding with each flashback .... I am beginning to feel more and more comfortable now and know that the past has no influence on me in the present .... while continuing to view the root of my fear ...... I let the screen come a little closer to me .... at a comfortable distance from me .... and now I begin to let go and release old emotional ties to my fear .... the ties to my past .... the anxiety .... and the pain associated with my fear .... and as I release old emotional ties to the past ......

I allow the screen to come closer and closer .... and the memories are losing their hold on me .... and now I am imagining a cord connected from the screen to me .... a cord that ties me to the past .... a cord that ties me to my fear .... now I am imagining cutting the cord to the screen .... I am cutting the cord to the screen and releasing myself from the past and the fear of flying .... the screen fades away and as it fades I begin to feel healing taking place .... healing from past fears and past experiences .... healing and soothing .... and from now I am free of my old fear .... I am completely free .... I no longer need my fear .... my fear of the flying has disappeared .... has completely disappeared .... it has lost hold on me .... it has lost its strength .... I am imagining how good my life will be without this fear .... I am Imagining feeling wonderful flying up above the clouds .... flying over the world with excitement ...... I am imagining the day my flight comes and my cases and bags are packed .... everything is in order .... and I am very excited ....

allowing myself to absorb the lovely feeling of the aeroplane and my holiday destination .... feeling good inside .... about to visit all the wonderful places I've always wanted to see .... and this is all because my old fear is gone .... and I am completely free

Now that my fear is gone I am looking at it and noticing that I am stronger .... and much more in control .... I am completely at ease and strong .... I am happy and smiling because my fear of flying has lost its strength .... I am confident .... very confident because I can face anything and I have amazing inner strength .... all I need to do whenever I feel anxious is to breath deeply .... relax and feel a powerful surge of strength within me .... I am capable and confident and in control .... fying is safe ...... and its nothing to be scared of .... flying enhances my experience .... and takes me to other parts of the world .... flying is enjoyable and restful .... I am secure and safe on a plane .... I can sit back and relax .... calm and relaxed .... I am completely free of any fear now and I will continue to experience this freedom today .... tomorrow ...... and in the future .... I am smiling and happy as I acknowledge my achievement .... I have confronted my fear ...... and now feel strong, confident and proud of myself .... I have conquered my fear of flying .... I will continue to enjoy my special place as a wonderful healing takes place .... a healing that flows through me completely .... and continuing to relax .... floating and drifting .... totally relaxed .... when I am ready to come back to awareness ......

I will count from one to five ...... and as I count from one to five .... I will begin to come back to full awareness ...... I will come back feeling completely relaxed ......

1 ....I am beginning to come back
2................... Coming up and relaxed
3................... I am aware of my normal surroundings
4................... I am beginning to open my eyes
5................... I come back feeling relaxed

FEAR OF FLYING AFFIRMATIONS

I like flying

- I look forward to flying
- I am calm when flying
- I enjoy taking long flights
- I relax when on planes
- I enjoy travelling
- I can travel anywhere in the world
- I am overcoming my fear of flying
- I am banishing my fear of flying
- I am releasing my fear of flying
- I am safe while flying
- I feel safe while flying
- I feel secure flying
- Flying comes naturally to me and I enjoy it
- I feel calm on the plane
- I have trust in the plane staff
- I feel at ease with everyday that passes
- I let go of my fear of flying
- My mind is calm while flying
- I am in control of my fear of flying
- I am free of my fear of flying

****

Chapter Twenty
Fear of Snakes

The phobia and fear of snakes is known as ophidiophobia. Is defined as an intense anxiety and dread of snakes. Snakes are often feared as many people find them unsightly, slimy unpredictable and almost disgusting. The slithering movement of a snake also makes it unsightly and makes people's skin crawl. Together with their ability to strike without any warning not to mention killing makes snakes very scary. Evidence suggests that people suffering from this phobia do not actually have any direct contact with snakes. The phobia is understandable as some snakes are very poisonous and can cause potential harm and death to humans.

Snakes have fangs and often people are scared of receiving a fatal snake bite. Severe fear of snakes can cause panic attacks, sweating, feeling faint, trembling, nightmares about snakes, breathlessness, dizziness, nausea, sickness, increased heartbeat, palpitations, and avoidance of places where snakes might be such as parks, forests, zoos. It's well known that the fear of snakes, like most phobias, has its roots in " Learned " thought patterns and that the cure lies in getting to and altering these thought patterns which relates to snakes and thereby removing the fear element of the individual's mind view of snakes.

Self-hypnosis has been successful in freeing people from snake phobia and completely overcoming their fears of snakes. By accessing the subconscious mind directly where your patterns of thinking and beliefs about snakes exist, self-hypnosis can eliminate these beliefs quickly and directly changing the way how you think and feel about snakes subconsciously and stopping you from reacting anxiously when you see a snake.

FEAR OF SNAKES SCRIPT

I will make myself as comfortable as I can ...... take a nice deep breath ...... close my eyes and begin to relax ..... just thinking about relaxing every muscle in my body ...... as I begin to focus attention on my breathing .....my awareness of everything around me will decrease..... letting all the tension drain from my head ...... I am beginning to drift into a state of deeper and deeper relaxation ..... enjoying this pleasant feeling while my mind slowly unwinds ...... I feel comfortable, warm and relaxed ...... now I think about the muscles in my neck ...... allowing this warm wave of relaxation to fill all the muscles in my neck ...... enabling my neck to feel comfortable and relaxed ...... I am feeling the waves of relaxation pass from my neck into my shoulders .... enjoying this warm feeling while drifting into a deeper and deeper level of relaxation .... this feeling of relaxation passes down through my shoulders to my arms reaching down to the tips of my fingers ...... my arms are now feeling tired and heavy as I sink into a deeper and deeper state of relaxation .... now my chest muscles are relaxed too and my stomach muscles ...... I focus on the gentle rise and fall of my stomach muscles as I slowly breath in and out .... now this warm relaxed feeling flows through my legs as I notice how relaxed my limbs have become ...... my mind has become totally still and deeply, deeply relaxed ...... I concentrate on how my body feels while I enjoy this deep state of relaxation .... I am feeling lighter and lighter ...... floating higher and higher into a deeper level of relaxation ...... I am now completely relaxed .... more relaxed than I have ever felt before ...... as I experience this beautiful feeling of peace and calm ...... I will just let go of my mind ...... drift, relax and drift ....

Now that I am totally, deeply relaxed and at peace with myself ...... I will imagine myself in my special place ...... this is a very special place for me ...... is very peaceful and calm and filled with tranquillity ...... being in my special place makes me very calm and relaxed .....

Now I imagine going back into my past ...... the time when I first experienced my fear drifting back and thinking about my fear .... the fear of snakes .... I imagine seeing snakes on a movie screen feeling comfortable and safe .... I bring the screen even more closer to me feeling more stronger and confident ...... I imagine myself face to face with all kinds and colours of snakes ...... I notice how cool and peaceful they are .... their beautiful colours and patterns ...... I accept that snakes are part of nature .... and they are not interested in harming me in any way ...... in fact they look friendly but scared of me .... and now I know that I have nothing to be scared of ...... the snakes are more scared of me than I am scared of them ...... because I am stronger than them ...... and they are very weak and I am more stronger than them ...... I am much stronger ...... I feel confident around snakes and in control of the situation .... and notice how relaxed I am beginning to feel around snakes .... I am at ease ...... completely at ease and strong ...... I realise that now I am in control of my fear and I am happy ...... I am happy because my fear has lost its strength .... I am confident because I can face snakes now .... I am confident and strong and whenever I feel anxious and fearful all I need to do is breath in and out and the anxiety will melt away ...... because I am confident and in charge ..... day by day I become more calm and in control .... and because I feel stronger and in control I will begin to let go of my fear ...... releasing all my emotional ties to my fear and allow myself to move forward releasing myself from the past .... I am free from my fear of snakes ..... I am completely free and feel very relieved and happy that my fear has gone ...... has completely left me ...... and this joyous feeling will stay with me in the many days to come.

I will enjoy my special place for another moment ...... take all those positive feelings in ...... and bring them back with me ..... drift and float ...... I am feeling calm and relaxed ......

In a few minutes when I am ready to come back to full awareness ...... I will count from one to ten .... and as I count from one to ten ...... I will begin to come back to full awareness ...... I will come back feeling at ease and relaxed ....

1.................... Beginning to come back
2.................... The background noises are coming back
3 ....Feeling relaxed
4.................... I am aware of my body
5 ....Calm and peaceful

6 ....I am almost fully alert now

7 ....Feeling relaxed

8 ....I am aware of my normal surroundings

9 ....Beginning to open my eyes now

10 ....I open my eyes and come back feeling wonderful

FEAR OF SNAKES AFFIRMATIONS

- I am overcoming my fear of snakes
- I am in control of my reaction to snakes
- I am calm around snakes
- I think about snakes calmly
- I am confident and fearless around snakes
- I work in my garden fearlessly
- I am cured of my fear of snakes
- My fear of snakes is gone
- Snakes are a part of nature
- My breathing is calm around snakes
- When I see snakes I am calm
- I like snakes
- I am not scared of snakes
- There is nothing to be scared of about snakes
- I accept that snakes are part of nature
- I am confident around snakes
- I choose to live fear free of snakes
- I am relaxed around snakes
- I let go of my fear of snakes
- I walk through the forests fearlessly
- I am in control of my reaction around snakes
- I react positively around snakes
- I am free of my fear of snakes

....

Chapter Twenty-One
Fear of Public Speeches

Fear of public speeches also known as glossophobia is the fear of public speaking or speaking in general. It is a common phobia ranging from slight nervousness to a vast amount of fear and panic. Many people with this phobia avoid speaking in public situations or go through them with shaking hands, fast heartbeat, breathlessness, sweating and a quavering voice. If not dealt with this fear can be career damaging and also cause unnecessary worry, stress and anxiety.

Glossophobia if not tackled can damage careers and lead to many sleepless nights. Together with hypnosis the following can also help you overcome your fear;

Know your topic and research it beforehand and consider questions that your audience may ask you and have your answers ready.
- Practice your speech as much as you can
- Practice deep breathing as it can be calming
- Focus on your material rather than your audience seeing that people will pay more attention to what you are presenting and probably wont even notice your nervousness!
- Get support- join a group that supports people who have difficulty with public speeches.
- Recognise your success- after the speech give yourself a pat on the back and don't be disheartened by any mistakes you have made, see those mistakes as opportunities to improve your skills.

Causes of fear of public speeches
- Lack of confidence
- Self consciousness
- Fear of making mistakes, saying the wrong thing, falling over, being laughed at
- Fear of being the centre of attention
- Fear of forgetting what to say

- Fear of criticism and being judged
- A traumatic event in the past which may be or not linked directly to public speeches.

The symptoms of fear of public speeches are; inability to speak, sweating, shortness of breath, shaking or trembling, nausea, rapid breathing, blushing, mental blocks, dry mouth, tight chest, feeling nervous, feeling embarrassed, feeling panicky, rapid heartbeat, tightness in throat and quavering voice.

FEAR OF PUBLIC SPEECHES SCRIPT

I will make myself as comfortable as I can ...... take a nice deep breath ...... close my eyes and begin to relax ..... just thinking about relaxing every muscle in my body ...... as I begin to focus attention on my breathing .....my awareness of everything around me will decrease..... as I feel all the tension drain from my head ...... I begin to drift into a state of deeper and deeper relaxation ..... I enjoy this pleasant feeling while my mind slowly unwinds ...... I feel comfortable, warm and relaxed ...... now I think about the muscles in my neck ...... allowing this warm wave of relaxation to fill all the muscles in my neck ...... enabling my neck to feel comfortable and relaxed ...... I am feeling the waves of relaxation pass from my neck into my shoulders and enjoying this warm feeling as I drift into a deeper and deeper level of relaxation ...... this feeling of relaxation passes down through my shoulders to my arms reaching down to the tips of my fingers ...... my arms are now feeling tired and heavy as I sink into a deeper and deeper state of relaxation .... now my chest muscles are relaxed too and my stomach muscles ...... I focus on the gentle rise and fall of my stomach muscles as I slowly breath in and out .... now this warm relaxed feeling flows through my legs as I notice how relaxed my limbs have become ...... my mind has become totally still and deeply, deeply relaxed ...... I concentrate on how my body feels while I enjoy this deep state of relaxation .... I am feeling lighter and lighter ...... floating higher and higher into a deeper level of relaxation ...... I am now completely relaxed .... more relaxed than I have ever felt before

...... as I experience this beautiful feeling of peace and calm ...... I will just let go of my mind ...... drift, relax and drift ....

Now that I am totally, deeply relaxed and at peace with myself ...... I will imagine myself in my special place ...... this is a very special place for me ...... it is very peaceful and calm and filled with tranquillity ...... being in my special place makes me very calm and relaxed ..... Now I think about my fear .... and tackling my fear .... the fear of public speaking .... I look back at all the anxiety and panic this fear has caused me ...... all the unnecessary worry and sleepless nights ...... and how great it would be to overcome my fear ..... for me to be able to give speeches in public with confidence and ease ...... for me to make a decision ...... to overcome my fear ...... starting today and now .... now I imagine myself getting ready to give a speech on one of my favourite topics ...... it is a topic that I am very passionate about and I really want to get my message across .... the day of my speech arrives and I feel very comfortable, relaxed and in fact excited about delivering my speech .... I picture myself having my turn and walking onto the podium to give my speech ...... I am standing at the podium now and I can see faces of people, some I know and who are friends and others I don't know but they all look friendly and interested in what I am going to say .... as I start giving my speech I am calm, relaxed and collected .... I am speaking up and nicely projecting my voice well .... everything I have prepared is coming to me .... all my ideas are flowing freely and nicely and I am finding myself relaxing and enjoying my speech even more as I go along ...... I am calm and concentrating on what I am saying .... I am breathing slowly and doing a wonderful job .... and as I continue to speak my fear decreases more and more .... I allow it to leave .... my fear has been weakened and I feel a great sense of relief and accomplishment .... and as I conclude my speech I feel in control and centred .... I breath in and out slowly feeling relaxed and confident ...... I summarise my speech feeling satisfaction of a job well done .... my audience are smiling and clapping their hands in appreciation and that feels wonderful .... I am happy and proud of myself for facing my fear .... I feel powerful, strong and in charge of my emotions .... from now on I will be able to deliver speeches effortlessly and with ease .... I will enjoy my speeches and look forward to giving them .... my fear has gone ....

I will enjoy my special place for another moment .... drift and float ...... I am feeling calm and relaxed ......   In a few minutes I will come back to awareness ...... I will count from one to ten .... and as I count from one to ten ...... I will begin to come back to full awareness ...... I will come back feeling relaxed ....

1....................Beginning to come back
2................... The background noises are coming back
3 ....Feeling relaxed
4.................... I am aware of my body
5 ....Calm and peaceful
6 ....I am almost fully alert now
7 ....Feeling relaxed
8 ....I am aware of my normal surroundings
9 ....Beginning to open my eyes now
10 ....I open my eyes and come back feeling wonderful

FEAR OF PUBLIC SPEECH AFFIRMATIONS

  I am a confident public speaker
- I am relaxed when speaking publicly
- I am at my best when speaking publicly
- I am positive about public speaking
- I am a great public speaker
- I always speak calmly and clearly
- I am a successful public speaker
- Others admire my ability to speak publicly
- I am at ease speaking in front of others
- I have confidence in myself
- I enjoy speaking to large crowds
- Each day I get better and better at public speaking
- I am relaxed in front of an audience
- People see me as someone who is a great speaker
- All fear and anxiety of public speaking is leaving my body and mind

I am a brilliant public speaker
I hear a roar of applause as I stand proud and confident in front of my audience
My message is clear and well received
I easily connect with the audience
I speak with confidence and power
I chose to be calm and relaxed in front of my audience
I am no longer scared of public speaking
I let go of my fear of public speaking
I am in control of my fear
I am a person just talking to other people
I am a successful public speaker
My fear of public speeches is in the past

....

Chapter Twenty-Two
Fear of Spiders

The fear of spiders is also known as Arachnophobia. It is estimated that there are one million arachnophobics in the United Kingdom. The fear of spiders is the most common specific phobia with 50% women and 10% of men showing symptoms of arachnophobia. People fear spiders because of their angular shaped legs, hairy bodies, dark colours, quick movements, which are unpredictable, their potential to harm or even as a learned habit. Different people suffer to different degrees from intense to mild, people with the fear of spiders will go to great length to avoid situations or areas they believe might harbour spiders, somewhat limiting their activities and life experiences. Symptoms of fear of spiders are; feeling anxious in places they are suspicious of spiders, worrying, trembling, trouble breathing, excessive sweating and rapid heartbeat.

An arachnophobic person has subconsciously linked feelings of anxiety with spiders. They have become conditioned to produce the fear response at the sight and sometimes thought of spiders. Often the actual phobia has been forgotten by the conscious mind and the person feels as if they have had this fear all their life, such however is not the case. The fear of spiders is something that is learned, not inborn. Self-hypnosis can reach the subconscious to where the conditioned fear is embedded and help eliminate it.

FEAR OF SPIDERS SCRIPT

I will make myself as comfortable as I can ...... take a nice deep breath ...... close my eyes and begin to relax ..... just thinking about relaxing every muscle in my body ...... as I begin to focus attention on my breathing .....my awareness of everything around me will decrease..... As I feel all the tension drain from my head ...... I begin to drift into a state of deeper and deeper relaxation ..... I enjoy this pleasant feeling while my mind slowly unwinds ...... I feel comfortable, warm and relaxed ...... Now I think about the muscles in my neck ...... allowing this warm wave of relaxation to fill all the muscles in my neck ...... enabling my neck to feel comfortable and relaxed ...... I am feeling the waves of relaxation pass from my neck into my shoulders and enjoying this warm feeling I drift into a deeper and deeper level of relaxation ...... The feeling of relaxation passes down through my shoulders to my arms reaching down to the tips of my fingers ...... my arms are now feeling tired and heavy as I sink into a deeper and deeper state of relaxation .... now my chest muscles are relaxed too and my stomach muscles ...... I focus on the gentle rise and fall of my stomach muscles as I slowly breath in and out .... Now this warm relaxed feeling flows through my legs as I notice how relaxed my limbs have become ...... my mind has become totally still and deeply, deeply relaxed ...... I concentrate on how my body feels while I enjoy this deep state of relaxation .... I am feeling lighter and lighter ...... floating higher and higher into a deeper level of relaxation ...... I am now completely relaxed .... more relaxed than I have ever felt before ...... as I experience this beautiful feeling of peace and calm ...... I will just let go of my mind ...... drift, relax and drift ....

Now that I am totally, deeply relaxed and at peace with myself ...... I will imagine myself in my special place ...... this is a very special place for me ...... it is very peaceful and calm and filled with tranquillity ...... being in my special place makes me very calm and relaxed .....

Now I think about my fear of spiders and all the misery and anxiety it has caused me in the past .... I realise I have to let go of this fear and set myself free from it ...... after all most spiders are harmless .... and spiders are part of nature and not looking to harm or injure anyone ...... spiders are calm and peaceful creatures ...... nothing to be feared at all ...... I have had so many achievements in the past and I know that I can make this positive change as well ...... of overcoming my fear of spiders ...... now I imagine going back into my past ...... the time when I first experienced my fear drifting back and thinking about my fear .... the fear of spiders .... I imagine seeing spiders on a movie screen feeling comfortable and safe ..... I bring the screen even more closer to me feeling more stronger and confident ...... I imagine myself face to face with all kinds, shapes and colours of spiders ...... I notice how calm and peaceful they are .... their vibrant colours and impressive shapes ...... they look small and weak to me ...... they are very weak and not scary at all I am more stronger than them ...... I am much stronger ...... I feel secure and in control of the situation and notice how relaxed I am beginning to feel around spiders .... I look into their eyes and reach out and touch one of them admiring its texture and shape ...... the spider seems to like my company and I am calm and relaxed ...... feeling just fine and at ease ...... completely at ease and strong ...... I realise that now I am in control of my fear and I am happy ...... I am happy because my fear has lost its strength .... I am confident because I can face spiders now without panicking and over reacting .... I am confident and strong and whenever I feel anxious and fearful all I need to do is breath in and out and the anxiety will melt away ...... because I am confident and in charge ..... day by day I become more calm and in control .... and because I feel stronger and in control I begin to let go of my fear ...... releasing all my emotional ties to my past fear of spiders and allow myself to move forward releasing myself from the past and healing .... I am free from my fear of spiders ..... I am completely free and this feeling will stay with me ......

I will enjoy my special place for another moment ...... take all these positive feelings in ...... and bring them back with me ..... drift and float ...... I am feeling calm and relaxed ......

In a few minutes when I am ready I will come back to awareness ...... I will count from one to ten .... and as I count from one to ten ...... I will begin to come back to full awareness ...... I will come back feeling calm and relaxed ....

1.................... I am beginning to come back
2.................... The background noises are coming back
3 ....I am feeling relaxed
4.................... I am aware of my body
5 ....Calm and peaceful

6 ....I am almost fully alert now
7 ....Feeling relaxed
8 ....I am aware of my normal surroundings
9 ....Beginning to open my eyes now
10 ....I open my eyes and come back feeling completely
   relaxed

FEAR OF SPIDERS AFFIRMATIONS

   I am calm around spiders
- I accept spiders as part of nature
- I am cured of my fear of spiders
- Arachnophobia is no longer part of me
- I feel safe near spiders
- Spiders are part of nature
- I am in control around spiders
- I am free of my fear of spiders
- I am free to live a normal life
- I think about spiders calmly
- I am fearless around spiders
- I am confident around spiders
- With each day I let go of my fear
- I am more and more relaxed near spiders
- Spiders are a harmonious part of nature
- I can easily calm myself around spiders
- I have perfect control over my reaction to spiders
- I am in control of my reactions around spiders
- I am beginning to accept and like spiders
- I think about spiders calmly
- I am not scared of spiders
- There is nothing to be scared of about spiders
- My fear of spiders is in the past
- I have overcome my fear of spiders
- I am free of my fear of spiders

****

Chapter Twenty-Three
Fear of Heights

The fear of heights or Acrophobia can range from a fear when on the top floor of a very tall building to fear of standing on a chair. People with this fear feel a sense of panic when they are at certain heights and often become unable to trust their sense of balance.

Fear of heights can be caused by early traumatic experiences, these experiences might include falling from a tree or witnessing someone get hurt from falling from a high place.

Acrophobia can also be transferred from parents to their children, children of acrophobic parents are more likely to be acrophobic themselves. Acrophobia however is so common that it may have a genetic component. Heights are a reasonable danger for people to fear, most people suffer from some degree of acrophobia and feel some discomfort, such as standing at a very high cliff edge.

Hypnosis can help some people if they;

- Can't even climb the stairs
- Go into tall buildings
- Driving near a drop, cliff, valley and so forth
- Too afraid to fly
- Going up a ladder
- Afraid of bridges, mountains
- Looking down a stairway
- Watching a television programme or film involving heights

Self-hypnosis can help you in overcoming the fear of heights by retraining your subconscious mind, because hypnosis bypasses the conscious mind and creates an alternative state of consciousness in which attention is focussed away from the present reality, attention can then be focussed towards particular images, thoughts, feelings, motivations and behaviours which will help change the conditioned responses and learned behaviours. Once treated you will be able to see the perceived threat or danger of heights in a more rational way.

FEAR OF HEIGHTS SCRIPT

I will make myself as comfortable as I can .... starting by concentrating on my breathing .... close my eyes and begin to relax every muscle in my body .... from the top of my head to the tips of my toes ...... as I concentrate on my breathing .... I am beginning to notice that all the everyday noises around me are starting to fade into the background ...... helping me to relax deeper and deeper......... more deeply relaxed than I have ever felt before.

I am letting all the muscles in my body relax   ...... starting with the muscles in my face .... letting them relax ...... relaxing the muscles around my eyes and my neck .... this feeling travels nicely and gently into my shoulders .... the wave of relaxation travels on through my arms and fingers .... and into my chest .... my breathing is deeper......... and slower focussing on the relaxation that my body is experiencing .... and realising just how good this feels .... now the relaxation is going down into my stomach .... it's very calm and peaceful .... and the feeling has reached my hips now .... very slowly travelling down my legs .... into the large muscles in my thighs .... and then down into my feet .... feeling them with total relaxation .... I notice that this feeling of total relaxation has filled every part of me with peace and tranquillity .... I am now feeling deeply and completely relaxed .... just letting my mind drift .... relax and drift .... deeper and deeper ....

Now that I am deeply and completely relaxed ...... I am imagining myself in my special place .... the most relaxing and peaceful place for me .... in this place no one wants anything from me .... its just me .... time for myself to relax and enjoy .... in this place my body relaxes deeper and deeper .... and mind becomes calmer and calmer .... I am feeling lighter and lighter .... floating higher and higher into a comfortable relaxation .... I feel wonderful inside and out .... I am completely relaxed and ecause I am so relaxed .... I am imagining reaching my goal of overcoming my fear of flying .... my subconscious is completely ready to listen .... and to absorb everything ...... I will let my mind drift back in time .... and as I begin to drift easily back in time .... I know that I am safe and secure and in control and can always stop at any time .... I will continue to drift back in time and let my mind think about my fear .... the fear of heights .... my phobia that frightens me .... I will let my mind go back in time where my fear started .... knowing that here and now I am safe and secure .... going back to the first time I experienced my fear of heights .... I can see it at a distance ...... viewing everything on the screen as a movie....... at a safe distance .... I am feeling fine and calm .... I begin to understand why I felt fearful of heights .... as I gain more understanding with each flashback .... I begin to feel more and more comfortable now and know that the past has no influence on me in the present .... while continuing to view I let the screen come a little closer to me .... at a comfortable distance from me .... and now I begin to let go and release old emotional ties to my fear of heights ...... the anxiety this fear has caused me and the pain associated with this fear .... and as I release old emotional ties to the past ...... I allow the screen to come closer and closer .... and the memories start to loose their hold over me .... and now I am imagining a cord connected from me to the screen .... a cord that ties me to my past .... a cord that ties me to my fear ..... now I am imagining cutting the cord to the screen .... I am cutting the cord to the screen and releasing myself from the past and the fear of heights ..... the screen fades away and as it fades I begin to feel healing taking place .... healing from past fears and past experiences .... healing and soothing .... and from now I am free of my old fear .... I am completely free .... I no longer need my fear .... my fear of heights has disappeared .... it has completely disappeared ...... it has lost hold on me .... it has lost its strength .... and now I am imagining how good my life will be without this fear ...... I imagine myself approach a very tall and magnificent building ...... I see myself approaching it calmly and there is a glass elevator which runs up the side of the building .... giving me a stunning view of the surrounding areas and I see myself get into the elevator and begin to go up slowly ...... safely, confidently and relaxed .... I notice passing the 1st, 2nd, 3rd, 4th, 5th, 6th, 7th, 8th, 9th and 10th floors .... feeling very comfortable and in control as I watch the numbers continue to go higher and higher .... in fact the higher we go the more enjoyable and comfortable it feels ...... feeling more and more relaxed enjoying the beautiful view ...... now the elevator has reached the top floor ...... the 30th floor .... I now exit the elevator and walk on the roof and there is a very safe and secure railing going all around the roof .... and I walk to the other side of the roof and I look over the edge comfortably feeling calm and relaxed ...... feeling just fine ...... and I realise that the more I stay up here the more calm and relaxed I become ...... it feels all natural to me, my body is so relaxed and my mind is drifting and floating .... and from now and onwards I will continue to experience this feeling when I am in high places .... I allow myself to absorb this lovely feeling .... and now that my fear is gone I am feeling stronger and stronger .... and much more in control .... I am completely at ease and strong .... I am happy and smiling and proud of myself .... proud of my achievement .... I am very confident because I can face anything and I have amazing inner strength .... all I need to do whenever I feel anxious is to take a deep breath .... and feel a powerful surge of strength and relaxation flowing through me .... I am capable and confident and in control ... I am free of my fear of heights ...... completely free.

I will continue to enjoy my special place as a wonderful healing takes place .... a healing that flows through me completely .... continuing to relax .... floating and drifting ....totally relaxed .... In a few moments I will come back to awareness by counting from one to five ...... and as I I count from one to five .... I will begin to come back to full awareness ...... and at the count of five I will open my eyes and come back feeling completely relaxed ......

1 ....Beginning to come back
2.................. Coming up and relaxed
3.................. I am aware of my normal surroundings
4.................. I am beginning to open my eyes
5.................. I open my eyes and come back feeling relaxed

FEAR OF HEIGHTS AFFIRMATIONS

I am in control of my thoughts
- I enjoy the view from heights
- I am calm when I am high up
- I am relaxed on high places
- I enjoy the view from tall buildings
- I am confident being high up
- I am comfortable being in a high place
- I have overcome my fear of heights
- I enjoy looking down from heights
- My mind is always calm
- I will lead a fear-free life
- Heights are no longer a problem for me
- Being high up comes naturally to me
- I let go of my fear
- The views from heights are magical
- I embrace heights
- I am no longer scared of heights
- I am in control of my thoughts and actions
- I love being high up
- My fears are gone for good
- I am fearless in high places
- I am now free of the fear of heights
- I put fear in its place and myself back in control
- I choose to live without fear
- I am free of the fear of heights
- My fear of heights is gone and is in the past

....

Chapter Twenty-Four
Fear of Confined Spaces

The fear of confined spaces or claustrophobia is an anxiety disorder, it affects 10% of the UK population, people with claustrophobia react with mild or extreme anxiety in confined spaces, the sufferer has an irrational fear of having no escape or being closed in. It frequently results in panic attacks and can be triggered by certain situations, for example being in an elevator, room without windows or sitting in an aeroplane. People with claustrophobia can find the disorder hard to live with as they go to great lengths to avoid small spaces and situations which trigger their fear.

Causes of claustrophobia

Claustrophobia is generally a result of an experience in the person's past usually in their childhood that had led them to associate small spaces with the feeling of panic or being in imminent danger. Examples of such experiences are;

- Being locked in a cupboard, dark room, basement, attic
- Falling into a deep pool and not being able to swim
- Being in a crowded area and getting separated from parent or group
- Crawling into a hole and getting lost or stuck
- Being involved in an accident where doors or windows won't open such as in a train, bus, car, airplane, building

As the experience will have dealt some kind of trauma to the person, it will affect their ability to deal with similar situations rationally. The mind links the small or confined spaces to the feeling of being in danger and the body reacts accordingly, how it thinks it should react. This type of cause is termed as classic conditioning and can also be a behaviour inherited from parents. For instance a child observing their parents' reactions and behaviour develop the same fear. Symptoms of claustrophobia are sweating, fast heart rate, increased blood pressure, shaking, headaches, panic attacks, nausea, fainting, fear of actual harm or illness, and irritability.

The following are examples of how a claustrophobic sufferer may behave;

1- They may urgently check out the exits of the room as soon as they get in and position themselves as near as possible to the exit.

2- Avoid driving during busy times when traffic is likely to be congested.

3- If the venue is in a large and spacious room at a crowded event, they will be at the nearest door, when all doors are closed they may feel trapped and troubled.

4- They may avoid travelling as a passenger in a car, bus or train during peak times.

5- In severe cases, some people with this fear may have a panic attack when the door is closed.

6- They will avoid using elevators and use the stairs, even when this means getting tired and breathless.

Through self-hypnosis claustrophobia can be successfully be treated by allowing you to view your experiences subconsciously and thereby helping you to develop a new perspective that does not hold the fear that was programmed into you by earlier experiences. Self-hypnosis re-programmes the mind with positive ways of thinking and hence getting rid of the negative patterns of thinking behaviour.

FEAR OF CONFINED SPACES SCRIPT

I will make myself as comfortable as I can ...... take a nice deep breath ...... close my eyes and begin to relax ..... just thinking about relaxing every muscle in my body ...... as I begin to focus attention on my breathing .....my awareness of everything around me will decrease ..... feeling all the tension drain from my mind ...... I begin to drift into a state of deeper and deeper relaxation ..... I enjoy this pleasant feeling while my mind slowly unwinds ...... I feel comfortable, warm and relaxed ...... now I think about the muscles in my neck ...... allowing this warm wave of relaxation to fill all the muscles in my neck ...... enabling my neck to feel comfortable and relaxed ...... I am feeling the waves of relaxation pass from my neck into my shoulders and enjoying this warm feeling I drift into a deeper and deeper level of relaxation ...... this feeling of relaxation passes down through my shoulders to my arms reaching down to the tips of my fingers ...... my arms are now feeling tired and heavy as I sink into a deeper and deeper state of relaxation .... now my chest muscles are relaxed too and my stomach muscles ...... I focus on the gentle rise and fall of my stomach muscles as I slowly breath in and out .... now this warm relaxed feeling flows through my legs as I notice how relaxed my limbs have become ...... my mind has become totally still and deeply, deeply relaxed ...... I concentrate on how my body feels while I enjoy this deep state of relaxation .... I am feeling lighter and lighter ...... floating higher and higher into a deeper level of relaxation ......

I am now completely relaxed .... more relaxed than I have ever felt before ...... as I experience this beautiful feeling of peace and calm ...... I will just let go of my mind ...... drift, relax and drift ....

Now that I am totally, deeply relaxed and at peace with myself ...... I will imagine myself in my special place ...... this is a very special place for me ...... it is very peaceful and calm and filled with tranquillity ...... being in my special place makes me very calm and relaxed ..... Now that I am completely at ease and relaxed ...... I imagine going back into my past ...... the time when I first experienced my fear ...... drifting back and thinking about my phobia .... the fear of confined spaces .... I imagine myself approaching a building, car, train, bus, an elevator, airplane, whatever my fear is ...... and how this fear started or what triggered it .....

I view my past experience with my fear of confined spaces at a safe distance as an spectator ..... I know I am in control and can stop any time I want to ...... I have had so many successes in the past and I know I can do this as well because of my strength and capability ...... I go back in time and let my mind drift and float freely ...... and see the first time I experienced my fear ...... I begin to understand why I felt fearful ..... the more I see the more understanding I gain ...... and the less fearful I become ..... as I learn about my past I let my mind and body relax even more ...... releasing all the fear and anxiety .... I begin to feel my fear losing its strength ...... while I am getting stronger and stronger ...... I can feel healing taking place and releasing me from my past fear of confined spaces ..... my body and mind feel free and safe now with all the fear gone ...... I feel completely free and I will continue to experience this freedom ...... I know I can do anything that I want to do .... I feel strong and safe ...... now I that I am even more relaxed and comfortable I imagine getting into any building, elevator, airplane, or car ...... in a confined space ...... small space .... feeling calm and relaxed ...... without being anxious .... without any fear ...... because I am confident and secure in myself and my capabilities ......I realise that I am relaxed and okay with confined spaces ...... I can feel my fear and anxiety evaporating ...... and fading away ...... away from me .... in fact the more time I spend in enclosed spaces the more I feel strong and in control ...... I am smiling and proud of myself for achieving my goal ...... and it feels so good .... I feel free of my fear and let all go of all my emotional ties to confined spaces ......

I let my fear go ..... my past go ...... from this day on I will feel safe, relaxed and comfortable with small spaces ...... I am free ...... completely free ......I will enjoy my special place for a few more minutes ...... continue to relax ..... drift and float ...... I am feeling calm and relaxed ...... and when I am ready to come back to full awareness ...... I will count from one to ten .... and as I count from one to ten ...... I will begin to come back to full awareness ...... I will come back feeling at ease and relaxed ....

1...................Beginning to come back
2.................... The background noises are coming back
3 .... Feeling relaxed
4.................... I am aware of my body
5 .... Feeling calm and peaceful
6 .... I am almost fully alert now

7 ....Feeling relaxed
8 ....I am aware of my normal surroundings
9 ....Beginning to open my eyes now
10 ....I open my eyes and come back feeling wonderful

FEAR OF CONFINED SPACES AFFIRMATIONS

I am always relaxed and at ease
I am calm in elevators
I am overcoming claustrophobia
I am fearless in small spaces
I am calm on trains
I am calm and relaxed on buses
I am calm in crowded rooms
I am in control of myself in confined spaces
I breath easily in small spaces
I am safe in confined spaces
I am comfortable in new places
I am perfectly fine being in a small room
I am overcoming my fear
I am in control of my fear
I feel safe in elevators
I feel safe on public transport
Tight places don't scare me anymore
Small places feel comfy
I am no longer a claustrophobic
I choose how I react in small places
I choose to react relaxed and calmly
I am just fine in large crowds
My fears have melted away
I have let go of my fear of confined spaces
I am free of worrying
I am strong and in control
I am confident in small spaces
Claustrophobia is no longer part of me
I am the master of my actions
I choose to be free of claustrophobia

Chapter Twenty-Five
Fear of Public/Open Places

Fear of public places or open places also known as Agoraphobia is an intense fear of being in public places, being in areas with no easy reach, being in unfamiliar place or leaving your home. The severity of agoraphobia can vary significantly between different people, for example someone with extreme agoraphobia may not be able to leave their home at all whereas someone with mild agoraphobia may be able to travel short distances from home without problems. People with severe agoraphobia will avoid situations where they have to leave the house.

Causes of agoraphobia

Panic disorder- is an anxiety disorder characterized by recurring panic attacks
- Social phobia- an anxiety disorder whereby a person has an excessive fear of social places
- Post-Traumatic Stress Disorder- an anxiety disorder caused by very stressful, frightening and distressing life events like such as bereavement, illness, divorce
- Biological reasons- agoraphobia can be hereditary with children of parents who sufferer from agoraphobia being at high risk of suffering from it.
- Other phobias like fear of confined spaces may contribute to agoraphobia.

Symptoms of agoraphobia

Agoraphobia symptoms can be classified into 3 types;

Physical, Cognitive and Behavioural

1- Physical symptoms are:
- Rapid heartbeat
- Rapid breathing
- Feeling hot

- Feeling sick
- Upset stomach
- Chest pain
- Difficulty swallowing
- Diarrhoea
- Trembling
- Dizziness
- Feeling faint

2- Cognitive symptoms may include fear of:
- Inability to escape from a place
- Losing sanity
- Losing control in public
- Trembling in front of people
- Being stared at
- Looking stupid and embarrassed in case of panic attack in front of people

3- Behavioural symptoms are:
- Avoiding situations that could lead to panic attacks such as crowded places, public transport, and queues.
- Not being able to leave the house for long periods of time
- Needing to be with someone you trust when going any where
- Avoiding being far away from home.

Self-help tips for agoraphobia management

- Learning and practicing breathing and relaxation techniques to keep panic attacks at bay and alleviate feelings of anxiety.
- Confront your fears
- Get information on your condition and educate yourself on changes you can make in your lifestyle
- Reduce stress because the main source of anxiety is stress.
- Enrol yourself on online support groups where you can get important information and coping skills from other members.

Research has indicated that hypnosis can provide lasting relief from the symptoms of agoraphobia. Agoraphobia can occur when a panic attack disorder is left untreated and gets to the point where the sufferer is terrified to leave the home for fear of having severe panic attacks. Self-hypnosis can help you to deal with your mind because it's responsible for your thoughts, habits, attitudes and beliefs. If you can change your mind then you can do just about anything.

AGORAPHOBIA SCRIPT

I will make myself as comfortable as I can ...... take a nice deep breath ...... close my eyes and begin to relax ..... just thinking about relaxing every muscle in my body ...... as I begin to focus attention on my breathing .....my awareness of everything around me will decrease..... as I feel all the tension drain from my head ...... I begin to drift into a state of deeper and deeper relaxation ..... I enjoy this pleasant feeling while my mind slowly unwinds ...... I feel comfortable, warm and relaxed ...... now I think about the muscles in my neck ...... allowing this warm wave of relaxation to fill all the muscles in my neck ...... enabling my neck to feel comfortable and relaxed ...... I am feeling the waves of relaxation pass from my neck into my shoulders, and enjoying this warm feeling I drift into a deeper and deeper level of relaxation ...... the feeling of relaxation passes down through my shoulders to my arms reaching down to the tips of my fingers ...... my arms are now feeling tired and heavy as I sink into a deeper and deeper state of relaxation .... now my chest muscles are relaxed too and my stomach muscles ...... I focus on the gentle rise and fall of my stomach muscles as I slowly breath in and out .... now this warm relaxed feeling flows through my legs as I notice how relaxed my limbs have become ...... my mind has become totally still and deeply, deeply relaxed ...... I concentrate on how my body feels while I enjoy this deep state of relaxation .... I am feeling lighter and lighter ...... floating higher and higher into a deeper level of relaxation ...... I am now completely relaxed .... more relaxed than I have ever felt before ...... as I experience this beautiful feeling of peace and calm ...... I will just let go of my mind ...... drift, relax and drift ....

Now that I am totally, deeply relaxed and at peace with myself ...... I will imagine myself in my special place ...... this is a very special place for me ...... it is very peaceful and calm and filled with tranquillity ...... being in my special place makes me very calm and relaxed .....

Now I imagine going back into my past ...... the time when I first experienced my fear drifting back and thinking about my phobia....... the fear of public places .... the fear of open places .... the fear to leave my home .... this fear has caused me so much anxiety and has prevented me to leave my home .... It has kept me a prisoner .... I imagine losing my fear and myself leaving my house and approaching whatever my fear is ...... being in public places ...... or being on public transport and that feels fine ..... I look back into my past to find out how this fear started and what triggered it ..... I view my past experience of my fear of public places at a safe distance as a spectator ..... I know I am in control and can stop any time I want to ...... I know I am strong enough and can do this ...... because of my strength and capability ...... I go back in time and let my mind drift and float freely ...... and see the first time I experienced my fear ...... as I look further into my past I gain even more understanding and why I felt fearful ..... and what has been causing me all the anxiety and panic ..... the more I learn about my past the less fearless I become ...... I let my mind and body relax even more ...... releasing all the fear and anxiety .... my fear is losing its strength and I am getting stronger and stronger ......

I can feel healing taking place and releasing me from my past fear of public places ...... my body and mind feel free and safe now with all the fear leaving me ...... I will always relax my body whenever I feel fear or panic building inside me ...... I will breath deeply in, into my belly, and then let go of everything as I exhale ...... whenever I feel anxious I will take slow deep breaths into my abdomen and then breath out and relax my body ...... and my fear and panic will pass quickly .... and it will be over ...... from now on this will be my response to my fear and panic ...... I will no longer scare myself with anxious thoughts because I can cope and my fearful thoughts are fading fast ..... fading away .... and I am becoming stronger and stronger and more confident ...... with my new way of coping with my fear ...... I feel completely free and I will continue to experience this freedom ...... in the days to come ...... I know I can do anything that I want to do .... I feel strong and safe ...... Now that I am feeling even more stronger and relaxed .... I imagine myself leaving my house ...... going into a crowded and packed place ...... getting on a bus or train .... and that feels just fine .... just fine .... because I am confident and able to cope with my feelings ...... now I am able to calmly and confidently do all these things .... go to places I was scared to go .... I am able to leave my house and venture into situations that made me anxious before ...... I can go wherever I want and I can do whatever I want to do ...... I have new abilities to cope and I am free .....I realise that I am relaxed and okay with open spaces ...... I can feel my fear and anxiety evaporating ...... in fact the more time I spend in public places the more I feel strong and in control ...... I am smiling and proud of myself for achieving my goal ...... and it feels so good .... I feel free of my fear and let go of all my emotional ties to my fear ...... I let my past go ..... from this day on I will feel safe, relaxed and comfortable with wherever I choose to go ...... I am free ...... completely free ......

I will enjoy my special place for another moment ...... enjoy these positive feelings ...... and bring them back with me into the future .... I will continue to relax ...... drift and float ...... I am feeling calm and relaxed ...... and when I am ready to come back to full awareness ...... I will count from one to ten .... and as I count from one to ten ...... I will begin to come back to full awareness ...... I will come back feeling relaxed ....

1.................... Beginning to come back
2.................... The background noises are coming back
3 ....Feeling relaxed
4.................... I am aware of my body
5 ....Calm and peaceful
6 ....I am almost fully alert now
7 ....Feeling relaxed
8 ....I am aware of my normal surroundings

146

9 ....I am beginning to open my eyes now

10 ....I open my eyes and come back feeling wonderful

AGORAPHOBIA AFFIRMATIONS

I am safe outside

I am confident in public places

I enjoy being in public places

I am calm in social situations

I am free to go anywhere

I am safe in public places

I am confident in new places

I am free from agoraphobia

I release my fears

I let go of my fears

I am a confident person

I am in charge of my thoughts

I choose to think only positive thoughts

I am overcoming my fear

I enjoy leaving my house with each day

I am enjoying meeting new people

I enjoy visiting new places

I am calm and relaxed outdoors

Open places feel safe

I feel calmer than ever before

I have peace of mind

I am in control of my fear

I love the outdoors

I am free of my fear and anxieties

....

Chapter Twenty-Six
Fear of the Dark

Fear of the dark also known as Nyctophobia is one of the most common phobias in children. The fear is usually associated with dangers concealed by the dark other than the darkness itself. This fear is common in children and passes when they get older, however most people retain some form of fear of the dark as a form of survival instinct to be alert to the natural dangers of darkness. In many cases, childhood fears of the dark pass as the child matures. However this fear can become unhealthy with frequent panic attacks, sleepless nights and nightmares. In severe cases the sufferer may avoid being in the dark, sleeping by themselves and even sleep with the lights on.

Causes of fear of the dark

Negative past experiences
- Fear of the unknown
- Media portrait of the dark such as in movies and events like Halloween
- Fear of dangers that might be lurking in the dark such as monsters, beasts, predators, vampires, ghosts and so forth
- Children of parents who are scared of the dark are more likely to pick the habit themselves.

Symptoms of fear of the dark are characterised with nervousness and anxiety in any darkened environment. People with extreme fear of the dark may only sleep at night with the lights on and may be reluctant to go out at night. Other symptoms also include sweating, increased heart rate, tightness of muscles, increased blood pressure, dilation of pupils- to let in more light, trembling and even illness when forced to spend time in the dark.

The only way to eliminate fear of the dark is to re-programme the subconscious mind under self-hypnosis. It is said that the conscious part of the mind accounts for about only 10% this is to say that if a person wills to make positive changes purely on a conscious level, they are bound to fail. By using self-hypnosis you will break free from negative patterns of behaviour and accept positive new conditions, which is why hypnosis is so effective in overcoming phobias and creating permanent positive changes.

FEAR OF THE DARK SCRIPT

I will make myself as comfortable as I can .... starting by concentrating on my breathing .... close my eyes and begin to relax every muscle in my body .... from the top of my head to the tips of my toes .... as I concentrate on my breathing ....I will begin to notice that all the everyday noises around me are fading into the background .... helping me to relax deeper and deeper........ more deeply relaxed than I have ever felt before ..... I will let all the muscles in my body relax .... starting with the muscles in my face .... letting them relax .... I will then relax the muscles around my eyes and my neck .... this feeling travels nicely and gently into my shoulders .... the wave of relaxation travels on through my arms and fingers .... and into my chest .... my breathing is deeper........ and slower focussing on the relaxation that my body is experiencing .... and realising just how good this feels .... now the relaxation is going down into my stomach .... its very calm and peaceful .... and I am finding that now the feeling has reached my hips .... very slowly travelling down my legs .... into the large muscles in my thighs .... and then down into my feet .... feeling them with total relaxation .... I notice that this feeling of total relaxation has filled every part of me with peace and tranquillity .... I am now feeling deeply and completely relaxed .... letting my mind drift .... relax and drift .... deeper and deeper ....

Still in this total feeling of relaxation and peace .... I am imagining myself in my special place .... I can smell the freshness of the air .... it's clean and fresh .... I can even see it .... its a place of beauty and tranquillity .... its my special place .... just for me .... I feel very calm and peaceful here .... and safe and secure .... I can feel my body relaxing even more .... deeper

149

and deeper .... enjoying these positive feelings .... the peace and calm .... I am feeling lighter and lighter .... floating higher and higher into a comfortable relaxation .... I am completely relaxed and because I am so relaxed .... I can imagine reaching my goal of eliminating all my fear of the dark.

I will let my mind drift back in time ...... and as I begin to drift easily, easily back in time ...... I see myself become younger and younger .... I know that I am safe .... I am protected by my own positive energy ...... I will view my past experiences as if I am a spectator ...... I am viewing my past experiences from a safe distance ...... I need only remember that I am in control ...... I can see past fears at a distance ...... I can see them up-close or I don't have to see them at all ...... if I choose to terminate the session .... all I need is count from one to ten and return to full consciousness .... however if I want to proceed .... I will just let the my mind drift back and think about my fear....... the fear of the dark ...... my phobia that frightens me .... and know that here and now I am safe ...... I am viewing myself as a detective .... I am curious and eager to learn about the route of my fear .... eager to investigate all the clues .... Now I am imagining myself back to the first time I experienced my fear ...... I see it at a distance .... I am imagining seeing it on a movie screen at a safe distance .... I am feeling fine

I am beginning to understand why I felt fearful .... small pieces of the puzzle are beginning to fit .... I am gaining more understanding with each recall .... I can clearly recall the incident that caused my phobia .... viewing the incident on the screen at a distance .... I am beginning to feel more comfortable and know the past has no influence on me in the present .... I am viewing the incident and beginning to understand why I became fearful .... as I learn about my past I let the screen come a little closer to me .... at a comfortable distance from me ...... and now I begin to let go and release old emotional ties to the past .... I am letting go of fear .... letting go of anxiety .... letting go of pain ...... as I release old emotional ties to the past ...... I allow the screen to come closer and closer .... and the memories are losing their hold on me ......

and when I am ready I will imagine a cord connected from me to the screen .... a cord that ties me to the past .... now I am imagining cutting the cord to the screen .... I am cutting the cord to the screen and releasing myself from the past .... just watching the screen fade away .... the screen grows more and more faint .... the screen is dim and disappearing .... and as the screen fades I am beginning to feel healing taking place .... healing from past fears and past experiences .... healing and soothing .... and now my body, my mind, my heart, and my whole self is free of my old fear .... I am completely free .... I have set myself free ...... I no longer need my fear .... my fear of the dark has disappeared .... just disappeared .... my phobia has lost its strength .... and now I am completely free and feel relieved .... as if a burden has been lifted from my shoulders .... I feel at ease and completely free .... my old fear is gone .... gone completely ...... and now I am completely free and I will continue to experience this freedom ...... now I am imagining myself face to face with the dark....... making it into something I can see .... I am looking at it and noticing how weak it is ...... it is very weak, very weak .... I am much stronger than it is .... much stronger .... In fact it is afraid of me because I am much stronger than it is .... much stronger

I am at ease, completely at ease ...... and strong ...... I am smiling because my fear has lost its strength .... I feel confident and strong....... very confident because I can face anything and I know that I have tremendous inner strength .... all I need to do whenever I feel anxious is to breath deeply .... relax, and feel a powerful surge of strength within me ...... smile and my stress will melt away ...... I am capable and confident and in charge .... I am imagining myself sleeping in my bed fear free .... feeling secure and safe in my bedroom .... be it day or at night .... and having a restful tranquil sleep .... fear free .... In fact the dark places around me are the same places that I can see in the daytime .... there is nothing to be fearful of .... these places are just put into shadow .... put into rest for a while .... darkness is a comfortable blanket that falls over everything .... darkness helps us relax .... It is a pleasant change from the full light of the day

.... it is part of nature .... we need the darkness because it helps us rest and sleep ....I will continue to enjoy my special place as a wonderful healing takes place .... a healing that flows through me completely .... continuing to relax .... floating and drifting ...... and when I am ready to come back to awareness....... I will count from one to five and as I count from one to five I will begin to come back to full awareness .... I will come back feeling relaxed ....

1.................... I am beginning to come back
2.................... Coming up
3.................... I am feeling relaxed
4.................... I am beginning to open my eyes
5.................... I open my eyes and come back feeling totally relaxed

FEAR OF THE DARK AFFIRMATIONS

I release my fear of the dark
- I am calm and relaxed in the dark
- Being in the dark is second nature to me
- I am in control of my fear of the dark
- I thrive in the dark
- I enjoy being in the dark
- Darkness is part of life
- Darkness aids sleeping
- I let go of my fear
- I have self control in the dark
- My mind is always calm in the dark
- I am no longer in fear of the dark
- I am fearless in the dark
- I am comfortable and relaxed in the dark
- I am just fine in the dark
- I have let go of my fear
- I find sleeping easy in the dark
- I love being in the dark
- Its relaxing and calming in the dark
- I am no longer scared of the dark
- I choose to be free of the dark

Chapter Twenty-Seven
Fear of Water

Fear of water or Aquaphobia is a common specific phobia. Like all phobias it may vary dramatically in severity from person to person. Some people are scared of deep water or strong waves or a mass of water such as oceans, seas, lakes while others fear swimming pools and bathtubs. Some are scared of getting in contact with water whereas others cannot even bear to look at a large body of water.

Aquaphobics always fear the worst which is drowning and will avoid activities involving water like swimming, boating, or even be anxious about water in the bathtub or shower.

Causes of Aquaphobia

The most common cause of aquaphobia is a previous negative experience, for example if a person has been through a near drowning, shipwreck or other scary occurrences in the water. The way that these experiences are handled plays a major role in determining whether a phobia will occur.

Symptoms of aquaphobia like all phobias vary between sufferers, the more severe symptoms will be shaking, freezing in a place or attempt to escape, anxiety, breathlessness, rapid heartbeat, dizziness, sweating and nausea.

The fear of water or aquaphobia is a learned or conditioned response. In this case the response most likely derives from some part of experience probably in childhood, which involved a person finding themselves struggling under water and feeling a sense of oncoming panic as their air supply was cut off. Or perhaps a person witnessed something similar happening to a loved one or close friend who may not have survived the incident. Either way whatever circumstances took place, the terror and shock of the experience imprinted itself on the subconscious which has since " learned" to associate water with the original terror and shock.

Through self-hypnosis this fearful memory-negative association can be ventilated and neutralized by easily " persuading" the subconscious to let go of its irrational attachment to exaggerated fears about water. Through this process the phobia about water either quickly or gradually disappears leaving you with a balance between a sensible respect of water to having no needless fear of it.

FEAR OF WATER SCRIPT

I will make myself as comfortable as I can ...... take a nice deep breath ...... close my eyes and begin to relax ..... just thinking about relaxing every muscle in my body ...... as I begin to focus attention on my breathing .....my awareness of everything around me will decrease..... as I feel all the tension drain from my head ...... I am beginning to drift into a state of deeper and deeper relaxation ..... I enjoy this pleasant feeling while my mind slowly unwinds ...... I feel comfortable, warm and relaxed ...... now I think about the muscles in my neck ...... allowing this warm wave of relaxation to fill all the muscles in my neck ...... enabling my neck to feel comfortable and relaxed ...... I am feeling the waves of relaxation pass from my neck into my shoulders and enjoying this warm feeling I drift into a deeper and deeper level of relaxation ...... this feeling of relaxation passes down through my shoulders to my arms reaching down to the tips of my fingers ...... my arms are now feeling tired and heavy as I sink into a deeper and deeper state of relaxation .... now my chest muscles are relaxed too and my stomach muscles ...... I focus on the gentle rise and fall of my stomach muscles as I slowly breath in and out .... now this warm relaxed feeling flows through my legs as I notice how relaxed my limbs have become ...... my mind has become totally still and deeply, deeply relaxed ...... I concentrate on how my body feels while I enjoy this deep state of relaxation .... I am feeling lighter and lighter ...... floating higher and higher into a deeper level of relaxation ...... I am now completely relaxed .... more relaxed than I have ever felt before ...... as I experience this beautiful feeling of peace and calm ...... I will just let go of my mind ...... drift, relax and drift ....Now that I am totally, deeply relaxed and at peace with myself ...... I will

154

imagine myself in my special place ...... this is a very special place for me ...... it is very peaceful and calm and filled with tranquillity ...... being in my special place makes me very calm and relaxed ..... Now I imagine going back into my past ...... the time when I first experienced my fear drifting back and thinking about my phobia....... the fear of water .... I imagine myself going back into the past ...... letting my mind drift back in time ..... and as I go back into time I view my fear and how this fear started or what triggered it ..... I view my past experience with my fear of water ...... at a safe distance as a spectator ...... I know I am in control and can stop any time I want to ...... I go back in time and let my mind drift and float freely ...... feeling more and more relaxed and drifting higher and higher into a deeper level of relaxation ...... now as I begin to view the first time I experienced my fear ...... I begin to understand why I felt fearful of water...... as I learn about my past and gain more understanding .... I let my mind and body relax even more ...... releasing all the fear and anxiety .... my fear is losing its strength and I am getting stronger and stronger ...... I can feel healing taking place and releasing me from my past fear of water ..... my body and mind feel free and safe .... from now on my fear of water will leave my mind and body ...... I feel completely free and I will continue to experience this freedom ...... I know I can do anything that I want to do .... I feel safe and secure...... there is nothing for me to be scared of ...... water is part of nature and harmless as long as I take the right precautions ...... I know I will always be safe in water ...... from now onwards I will feel safe in water ...... I will feel secure around water .... because I am more stronger, capable and confident .... now I see myself stepping into the water ....a swimming pool ..... feeling calm and relaxed ...... I am feeling just fine because I am in control and I always have the option to come out ...... in total control ...... without being anxious .... without any fear ...... because I am confident and secure in myself and my capabilities ...... I realise that I am relaxed and okay with water ...... I am smiling and confident because I am here to enjoy myself ...... I scope some water with my hands and apply it to my face and that also feels fine ..... and then I get into the water calmly and walk around enjoying the sensation of water flowing around my body ...... I can feel my fear and anxiety evaporating ...... in fact the more time I spend in the water the more I feel strong and in control ...... I am smiling and proud of myself ...... I have achieved my goal ...... and it feels so good .... being in water makes me calm ..... being around water is magical and freeing ...... the sound of water and pounding waves is very relaxing and soothing ..... the feeling of water on my skin is soothing .... because water is a purifier I feel clean, refreshed and energized .... swimming has great health benefits as it will help keep me fit ...... I can feel all the pains and aches in my body drift away into the water ...... my body feels light and healed in water and I feel wonderful .... my mind feels calm and at peace in water ...... I feel at one with nature and deeply calm in water ...... I am free from my fear and let go of all my emotional ties to water ...... I let my past go ..... from this day on I will feel safe, relaxed and comfortable in or around water ...... I am free ...... completely free ......I will enjoy my special place for another moment ...... take all these positive feelings in ...... and bring them back with me ..... drift and float ...... I am feeling calm and relaxed ......

And when I am ready to come back to awareness ...... I will count from one to ten .... and as I count from one to ten ...... I will begin to come back to full awareness ...... I will come back feeling relaxed.

1.................... Beginning to come back
2.................... The background noises are coming back
3 ....Feeling relaxed
4.................... I am aware of my body
5 ....Calm and peaceful
6 ....I am almost fully alert now
7 ....Feeling relaxed
8 ....I am aware of my normal surroundings
9 ....Beginning to open my eyes now
10 ....I open my eyes and come back feeling relaxed

FEAR OF WATER AFFIRMATIONS

I love water
- I enjoy swimming
- I feel calm in water
- I am a great swimmer
- I am at home near water
- I find water calming and relaxing
- I am in control of my emotions around water
- I feel safe in water
- I can swim easily in deep water
- I am letting go of my fear
- Water has a calming effect on me
- Being in water feels relaxing
- Being near water is calming
- Water is part of nature
- My fear of water is in the past
- I am confident in water
- I am confident near water
- Water relaxes and calms me down
- All my fears are gone
- I am fear free and strong
- I am just fine in water
- Swimming comes naturally to me
- I am at peace in water
- Swimming has a lot of health benefits for me
- My body and mind react positively in water
- I feel at peace and free in water
- I find water very relaxing, calming and soothing
- I choose to be free of my fear
- I am strong and capable of coping in water
- I am free from my fear of water

....

Chapter Twenty-Eight
Fear of Death

The fear of death also known as Thanatophobia is a very common phobia. It's normal to be scared of death because none of us knows what will happen to us after we die. Nevertheless to be extremely scared of death can be unhealthy and detrimental to our lives. If one fears death excessively, it can impact on their quality of life hence preventing them from enjoying life and appreciating it.

Types of death fears

- Fear of pain and suffering
- Loss of dignity and independence
- Fear of non-existence
- Fear of eternal punishment/judgement/hell- due to wrong deeds
- Loss of control and everything
- Fear of what will become of loved ones- very common in parents, single parents, and care givers
- Fear of how loved ones will cope financially after departure as well as the funeral costs

It's possible for the fear of death to be healthy when we fear death, we are more careful and behave more responsible and take precautions for example not smoking, taking drugs, excess alcohol consumptions, wearing seat belts, life jackets, not drink and driving, eating healthily, having health check ups, taking out life insurance cover and so forth. A healthy fear of death also reminds us to make the most of our time here and enjoy life to the full. It can also push us to work hard to leave a lasting and memorable legacy.

The world is not our permanent home but rather a place to experience and learn, the lessons we encounter as we go through life make us wiser as we grow older. Everything we acquire in life, for instance relationships, material things, power and even our bodies we leave behind. Its what we do in our lives that matters and the recollection of positive life experiences of love, courage, compassion, humility, courage, and joy that we take with us and what stays in the hearts of our beloved ones left behind. When we are sacred of death we ignore it by working for things that will be left behind, more so creating lots of negative energy hence wasting the opportunity to live life to the full and enjoy it. Nevertheless if we acknowledge death and not view it as a finality but accept it as a natural process or rebirth to the next level, we will value our lives more and view our time in the world as an opportunity to create as many positive actions as we can such as love, compassion, understanding, patience, kindness, empathy and by doing so creating more happiness and contentment within ourselves. Inevitably when our time comes to an end, we will be able to accept it and pass without fear, resentment, anger, guilt, regret, judging and our selves or blaming others. Because our minds will be empowered by all the good acts and positivity we've generated in our life time and also our conscience will be clean in other words making the end of our lives easy to face, accept and embrace.

Self-hypnosis for fear of death will help you to accept that death is inevitable so that you can make the most of life. It will re-programme your inner mind to allow you to appreciate death rather than dread death, in the process adding love to life and making living much more fulfilling, positive and meaningful.

FEAR OF DEATH SCRIPT

I will make myself as comfortable as I can .... starting by concentrating on my breathing .... close my eyes and begin to relax every muscle in my body .... from the top of my head to the tips of my toes ...... as I concentrate on my breathing ....I will begin to notice that all the everyday noises around me will fade into the background .... helping me to relax deeper and deeper......... more deeply relaxed than I have ever felt before .... I will let all the muscles in my body relax .... starting with the muscles in my face .... letting them relax .... I will then relax the muscles around my eyes and my neck .... this feeling travels nicely and gently into my shoulders .... the wave of relaxation travels on through my arms and fingers .... and into my chest

.... my breathing is deeper....... and slower focussing on the relaxation that my body is experiencing .... and realising just how good this feels .... now the relaxation is going down into my stomach .... its very calm and peaceful .... and I am finding that now the feeling has reached my hips .... very slowly travelling down my legs .... into the large muscles in my thighs .... and then down into my feet .... feeling them with total relaxation .... I notice that this feeling of total relaxation has filled every part of me with peace and tranquillity .... I am now feeling deeply and completely relaxed .... letting my mind drift .... relax and drift .... deeper and deeper ......

Still in this total feeling of relaxation and peace .... I am imagining myself in my special place .... I can smell the freshness of the air .... it's clean and fresh .... I can even see it in my special place in my mind .... its a place of beauty and tranquillity .... its my very special place .... just for me .... I feel very calm and peaceful here .... and safe and secure .... I can feel my body relaxing even more .... deeper and deeper .... enjoying these positive feelings .... the peace and calm .... I am feeling lighter and lighter .... floating higher and higher into a comfortable relaxation .... I am completely relaxed and because I am very relaxed .... I imagine reaching my goal of eliminating my anxiety of fear of death ...... for a while now I have been experiencing uncomfortable feelings ...... when I've been thinking about dying ...... and I know that I have to be grateful of my life ...... and also be able to accept that death is inevitable .... and that every living thing eventually dies at some point ...... to be able to live my life fully without worrying about dying ...... without letting my fear stop me enjoying life to the full ...... to be able to live in the present and utilise all the opportunities that come my way to the full ...... to stop my fear from ruining my life and causing un-necessary anxiety and worry ..... to understand that death is a natural human process that we all have to go through ...... to enter another chapter beyond this .... Now I will let my mind drift, float and relax .... and as I continue to drift easily and float ...... I am imagining myself in my final moments ...... the final days of my life

...... I imagine it being warm and lovely .... I am surrounded by all the people I love ..... surrounded by lots of love almost bathing in this sea of love ...... I feel just fine and happy and grateful that I have been blessed by all these lovely people in my life ...... I think about all the nice opportunities that have come way and all the achievements I have made .... and the good deeds and positive things I've done ...... the peoples' lives I've touched and those that have touched me ...... I feel so happy in myself and appreciative of the life I've had ...... I see why my life has played out the way it has ...... with good reason ...... and this makes me even more happy ..... my mind and body are at peace and calm ...... I feel accomplished that I have done all I had to do and its my time to go .... and that feels fine because I am ready and prepared ...... I have said all I have to say to everyone ...... given my thanks .... tied all loose ends and forgiven the people who wronged me ...... and have also asked for forgiveness for those I wronged ...... and that feels fine because I feel free and ready to go with a happy and light heart ..... and that feels just fine ..... life is a gift and I have embraced it ..... my fear of death has no impact anymore ...... and from now on I will live fearless releasing all my death anxiety because its no use ...... death doesn't scare me anymore I will go when I am ready ...... when I go it will be the right time for me to go and I will go in peace ...... I am at peace with death and will continue to be ..... from now on I will live in the present and enjoy my life to the full ...... I will live free from my fear of death as death is a natural process that cannot be stopped .... so not worth the anxiety and worrying .... I will always be calm thinking about death ...... I accept it for what it is ...... I am in charge of my thoughts and actions ...... I choose to think positively about death ...... and my anxiety and fear about death will fade away with each passing day .... I am finally free to live my life fully without any hang ups ...... I am releasing all my emotional ties to my fear of death ...... I am free of any anxiety ...... I feel a great sense of well-being and healing taking place though me .... I am feel in control, strong and confident ...... death doesn't scare me anymore .... I am free ......

I will continue to enjoy my special place as a wonderful healing takes place within my body and mind .... a healing that flows through me completely .... continuing to relax .... floating and drifting ..... In a few minutes when I am ready to come back to awareness .... I will count from one to five and as I count from one to five I will begin to come back feeling calm and relaxed.

1.................... I am beginning to come back
2.................... I am coming up
3.................... I am feeling relaxed
4.................... I am beginning to open my eyes
5.................... I open my eyes and come back all the way feeling
                wonderful

FEAR OF DEATH AFFIRMATIONS

  I am calm when thinking about death
- I am free from the fear of death
- I can speak easily and freely about death
- I am living life to the fullest
- Death is natural process
- I am not afraid of death
- I live for the present moment
- I am letting go of my fear of death
- I am calm at funerals
- I am in control of my thoughts
- I will lead a care free life
- I accept death and live to the fullest
- I am enjoying my life more than before
- I release my death anxiety
- I live fearlessly
- Thinking about death is not a big deal
- My fear of death is gone
- I embrace the cycle of life and death
- My attitudes towards death are positive
- Death is just the next stage of life
- Death signifies new beginnings
- I feel good inside and out

- Life is eternal
- I am open to understanding death
- I embrace life
- I am safe and always will be, even after I die
- I am open to living my life to its fullest
- My life on this earth will end when I am ready to leave
- I am ready to live and appreciate my life
- I am okay with dying
- Death doesn't scare me anymore
- I am at peace with death

....

Chapter Twenty-Nine
Fear of the Dentist

Fear of the dentist also known as dental phobia is one of the most suffered phobias among people. A British study suggested that four out of ten British people are afraid of visiting the dentist in one way or another, while an American study claims that it's between five out of ten in their group. Hence this shows that among all phobias and fears, the fear of the dentist is by far the highest in numbers. Fear of the dentist is caused by post traumatic stress disorder. A previous painful dentist experience might have been the trigger.

Not only a visit to the dentist causes such fear, but also a simple narration of a painful dentist event by someone can increase this fear. The fear of the dentist is caused by the invasive interventions like surgery -teeth extractions that the patient undergoes, the strong smells and lack of control. As a consequence the sufferer will only seek professional help when the problem has gotten out of control. It's very crucial that the patient relates with their dentist because a calm, caring and understanding dentist will lighten the experience and he will also put the patient at ease.

The symptoms of dental phobia are mental, emotional and physical;

Mental symptoms:
- Obsessive thoughts
- Difficulty thinking about anything other than fear
- Bad images of teeth
- Fear of losing control
- Fear of fainting

Emotional symptoms
- Anticipatory anxiety- persistent worrying about upcoming events involving teeth
- Terror- overwhelming fear of the pain
- Desire to free

Physical symptoms

- Dizziness, shaking, palpitations
- Shortness of breath
- Pounding heart
- Chest pain or discomfort
- Trembling
- Sweating
- Feeling of choking
- Nausea or stomach distress
- Faint feeling
- Numbness or tingling sensations
- Hot or cold flashes

Self-hypnosis will help you in overcoming dental phobia by relaxation, when you relax you cannot feel frightened. Being relaxed removes fear that is why people drink alcohol to stop fear, it relaxes them. In this relaxed state you can visualise in great detail going to the dentist feeling very relaxed, confident and without fear. Self-hypnosis suggestions also help in eliminating any fear and realigning the subconscious with reality so that you're free to resume your life in a normal and natural manner free of your dental anxiety with which you have lived for so long.

FEAR OF THE DENTIST SCRIPT

I will make myself as comfortable as I can ...... take a nice deep breath ...... close my eyes and begin to relax ..... just thinking about relaxing every muscle in my body ...... as I begin to focus attention on my breathing .....my awareness of everything around me will decrease..... as I feel all the tension drain from my head ...... I begin to drift into a state of deeper and deeper relaxation ..... I enjoy this pleasant feeling while my mind slowly unwinds ...... I feel comfortable, warm and relaxed ...... now I think about the muscles in my neck ...... allowing this warm wave of relaxation to fill all the muscles in my neck ...... enabling my neck to feel comfortable and relaxed ...... I am feeling the waves of relaxation pass from my neck into my shoulders and enjoying this warm feeling I drift into a deeper and deeper level of relaxation ...... this feeling of relaxation passes down through my shoulders to my arms reaching down to the tips of my fingers ...... my arms are now feeling tired and heavy as I sink into a deeper and deeper state of relaxation .... now my chest muscles are relaxed too and my stomach muscles ...... I focus on the gentle rise and fall of my stomach muscles as I slowly breath in and out .... now this warm relaxed feeling flows through my legs as I notice how relaxed my limbs have become ...... my mind has become totally still and deeply, deeply relaxed ...... I concentrate on how my body feels while I enjoy this deep state of relaxation .... I am feeling lighter and lighter ...... floating higher and higher into a deeper level of relaxation ...... I am now completely relaxed .... more relaxed than I have ever felt before ...... as I experience this beautiful feeling of peace and calm ...... I will just let go of my mind ...... drift, relax and drift ....

Now that I am totally, deeply relaxed and at peace with myself ...... I will imagine myself in my special place ...... this is a very special place for me ...... it is very peaceful and calm and filled with tranquillity ...... being in my special place makes me very calm and relaxed ..... Now I think about my fear of going to the dentist .... how it started and how it has affected my life .... I realise that going to the dentist has caused me a lot of un-necessary fear and anxiety in the past ...... dental procedures are for my own benefit and good ...... dentists are state approved professionals and know what they are doing .... there is nothing to be fearful for .... going to the dentist is good for my health and harmless ...... now that I am more relaxed and peaceful and more at ease with the idea of visiting my dentist ...... I will imagine going to my dental surgery safe and calm ......as I approach the surgery I am feeling even more and more relaxed and assured that everything will be just fine .... my dentist is a professional and he will do the best job possible ...... as I approach the surgery I can smell the hygienic smells which only further assure me that I am going to be just fine ...... getting all the treatments I need ...... all the care I need ...... as it's what I deserve ...... I check in and sit down in the waiting room for my turn feeling even more calm and relaxed ...... now my turn comes and I go into the treatment room still feeling very relaxed and in control ..... I sit in the dental chair taking notice of my dentist's caring nature and the comfortable dental chair .... and then I realise that this chair was designed to give as much comfort as possible ...... I also notice a light above me which relaxes me even more because of its warmth ...... I feel comfortable and peaceful and hardly feel any pain when the dentist is treating me ....my body is strong and able to cope with the small amount of pain I am feeling ...... I lie there drifting and floating higher into a deeper level of relaxation while I get all the care I need ...... I am surprised at how easily and quickly the treatment has gone ...... I am so proud of myself for going through it .... as I get out of the dental chair and out of the room I am smiling because I have done something good for myself ...... I am very happy that my fear of the dentist has diminished ...... my fear is in the past where it belongs ...... I am confident and strong now and will continue to be even stronger as time goes by .... free of my fear of the dentist ......

I will enjoy my special place for another moment ...... drift and float ......˙ I am feeling calm and relaxed ...... and when I am ready to come back to full awareness ...... I will count from one to ten .... and as I count from one to ten ...... I will begin to come back feeling calm and relaxed ....

1....................Beginning to come back
2....................The background noises are coming back
3 ....Feeling relaxed
4....................I am aware of my body
5 ....Calm and peaceful
6 ....I am almost fully alert now
7 ....Feeling relaxed
8 ....I am aware of my normal surroundings
9 ....Beginning to open my eyes now
10 ....I open my eyes and come back feeling wonderful

FEAR OF THE DENTIST AFFIRMATIONS
I am free from the fear of the dentist

- Its okay to talk about the dentist
- I choose to release my fears
- Everyday I release my fears
- I am fearless
- I am confident at the dentist
- My fear decreases each day
- I am fearless today and always
- I am free from fear of bodily injury
- I am in control of my thoughts and actions
- I put fear in its place and myself in control
- My health is more important to me
- I am comfortable and relaxed talking to my dentist
- I attend regular dental check ups
- I am cured of my fear of the dentist
- Dentists are healers
- Dentists make me feel safe
- My mind is calm around my dentist
- My dentist helps me keep healthy
- I appreciate my dentist
- I let go my fear
- I live a fear free and relaxed life
- My fear is in the past
- Going to the dentist doesn't scare me anymore
- I am always in control of my emotions
- My health matters to me more than my fear
- With each day I feel more confident going to the dentist
- I am a strong and capable person
- I am free of dental phobia

....

Chapter Thirty
Fear of Driving Tests

No one likes tests and exams, but the driving test seems to create the most anxiety for most many people. Despite the fact that you know you can drive competently, somehow it is impossible to feel confident about taking the actual driving test. And the fact is that the more nervous you get, the more likely you are to make mistakes. Worrying and thinking negatively about your test creates havoc with how you feel about the test. Many people feel so nervous that they fail again and again and again. Nevertheless some nervous anticipation is useful because it gives you the edge.

According to the Driving Standards Agency (DSA) the current overall pass rate for the driving test is just 42% and the first time pass rate is even lower, with 90% of the people believing that their negative thinking and nerves had a bad impact on their test results.

Self-hypnosis for fear of the driving test is designed to help you prepare mentally, to focus and relax before and during your driving test. Ideally success or failure starts in your mind.

FEAR OF DRIVING TEST SCRIPT

I will make myself as comfortable as I can ...... take a nice deep breath ...... close my eyes and begin to relax ..... just thinking about relaxing every muscle in my body ...... as I begin to focus attention on my breathing .....my awareness of everything around me will decrease ..... as I continue to breath in and out slowly ...... I begin to drift into a state of deeper and deeper relaxation ..... I enjoy this pleasant feeling while my mind slowly unwinds ...... I feel comfortable, warm and relaxed ...... now I think about the muscles in my neck ...... allowing this warm wave of relaxation to fill all the muscles in my neck ...... enabling my neck to feel comfortable and relaxed ...... I am feeling the waves of relaxation pass from my neck into my shoulders and enjoying this warm feeling I drift into a deeper and deeper level of relaxation ...... the feeling of relaxation passes down through my shoulders to my arms reaching down to the tips of my fingers ...... my arms are now feeling tired and heavy as I sink into a deeper and deeper state of relaxation .... now my chest muscles are relaxed too and my stomach muscles ...... I focus on the gentle rise and fall of my stomach muscles as I slowly breath in and out .... now this warm relaxed feeling flows through my legs as I notice how relaxed my limbs have become ...... my mind has become totally still and deeply, deeply relaxed ...... I concentrate on how my body feels while I enjoy this deep state of relaxation .... I am feeling lighter and lighter ...... floating higher and higher into a deeper level of relaxation ...... I am now completely relaxed .... more relaxed than I have ever felt before ...... as I experience this beautiful feeling of peace and calm ...... I will just let go of my mind ...... drift, relax and drift ....

Now that I am totally, deeply relaxed and at peace with myself ...... I will imagine myself in y special place ...... this is a very special place for me ...... it is very peaceful and calm and filled with tranquillity ...... being in my special place makes me very calm and relaxed .....

Now I imagine thinking about my fear .... the fear of driving tests and the un-necessary anxiety and nervousness it causes me .... tests are part of life and there is nothing to be fearful for ...... they are part of testing my knowledge and for my good and benefit .... they are just tests .... providing me with an opportunity to practice and recall ...... with no harm at all ...... driving is an essential part of life ...... being able to drive wherever I want to go with ease ...... the freedom of being able to drive myself and not rely on other people .... the independence that comes with driving ...... its an amazing feeling and a great achievement ...... and for my highest good and benefit ..... I have more to gain than to lose .... I imagine my driving test coming up very soon and I practice and get prepared for it .... the more I practice and revise the less anxious I feel about my driving test ...... I know I have given myself a big chance of passing it with all the preparation ...... because the art of passing a test is knowing what your examiner wants ....and I will pass it by practicing what the examiner will be looking for, relaxed and calmly .... the more I think about my test the more relaxed and confident I get .... now my test day arrives ..... I wake up feeling relaxed, calm and prepared for what's lying ahead ..... I know I will do well because I am well prepared .... I imagine myself getting into the test car with my examiner ...... feeling very relaxed, calm and at peace with myself with no nerves at all .... I start my test and I am focused and collected .... in fact I can remember everything that I revised and practiced ...... all the instructions are clearly given ...... and I make all the right manoeuvres and moves as we go along .... feeling more and more confident and relaxed the more I drive ..... I know most of the test route and very familiar with it .... and this gives me even more confidence .... I take one instruction at a time and I know that I will do well ...... I am able to remember all I have learned and recall the correct answers to the questions with ease because I am well prepared ...... I remember all the information I need ...... and as I conclude my test I know I have passed my test with ease .... I am very satisfied that I have done all the right moves and I am very proud of myself .... I am smiling all the way back to the test centre and I can see my examiner is satisfied and happy with my performance ...... at the test centre the examiner announces that I have passed my test .... I well-up with happiness and as I leave the examination room I feel a sense of pride and accomplishment flow through me ...... I am smiling because I have overcome my fear of the driving test ...... with tremendous courage and great strength ...... and from now on I will not be nervous and anxious when taking tests ...... anytime I feel nervous I will simply breath in and out and all the nervousness will fade away .... I know that I am strong and can overcome any obstacle that comes my way ...... I am free of my fear .... my fear is in the past ...... I am free ....I will enjoy my special place for a few more minutes .... drift and float .... feeling deeply relaxed and calm and when I am ready to come back to full awareness I will count from one to ten .... and as I count from one to ten ...... I will come back feeling completely relaxed.

1................I am beginning to come back
2................ The background noises are coming back
3 ....I am feeling relaxed
4................ I am aware of my body
5 ....Calm and peaceful
6 ....I am almost fully alert now
7 ....Feeling relaxed
8 ....I am aware of my normal surroundings
9 ....Beginning to open my eyes now
10 ....I open my eyes and come back feeling wonderful

FEAR OF DRIVING TEST AFFIRMATIONS

I am releasing all driving test fear
- I will sail through my driving test
- I am a confident driver
- I am a focused driver
- I am confident in my driving abilities
- I am staying calm during my driving test
- I am staying relaxed during my driving test
- I am enjoying my driving test
- I will pass my driving test
- Passing my driving test will come naturally for me
- I will concentrate on my driving
- I will be free of any fear during my test
- I will pass my driving test with ease
- I will thrive under the pressure
- I will enjoy my driving test
- I will be in control of my thoughts and actions during my test
- I believe in myself and my abilities
- I will pass my driving test
- I am very focused in my preparations
- My fears are in the past
- I am confident of passing my driving test
- I will be completely calm and relaxed during my driving test
- I will pass my driving test

****

Chapter Thirty-One
Fear of Exams

Examination fear, also know as Testophobia, is something that most students go through before the onset of examinations. Exams are a way of assessing what a student has learned during the academic year. However for most people exams bring a lot of tension, stress and anxiety because of increased pressure and high expectations from the students, parents, teachers and peers to perform well. Although a little bit of fear and anxiety is important to study and learn before the exams, too much tension can hamper the learner's ability to do well. To do well in exams you have to get over your anxiety and also have a positive mind set on passing. Many times, due to exam nerves and fear students tend to forget what they have learned, get confused, feel tense, dizziness, sleeplessness, lose appetite and feel blank hence scoring less than they could have scored. Therefore it is extremely essential for students to learn about how to reduce this fear, be able to relax and take their examinations confidently, subsequently earning good grades and passing them.

Lack of preparation will also hinder success, preparation should be done in advance by studying regularly and not leaving everything to the last minute which will create panic and more stress.

FEAR OF EXAMINATIONS SCRIPT

I will make myself as comfortable as I can ...... take a nice deep breath ...... close my eyes and begin to relax ..... just thinking about relaxing every muscle in my body ...... as I begin to focus attention on my breathing .....my awareness of everything around me will decrease ..... as I continue to breath in and out ...... I am beginning to drift into a state of deeper and deeper relaxation ..... I enjoy this pleasant feeling while my mind slowly unwinds ...... I feel comfortable, warm and relaxed ...... now I think about the muscles in my neck ...... allowing this warm wave of relaxation to fill all the muscles in my neck ...... enabling my neck to feel comfortable and relaxed ...... I am feeling the waves of relaxation pass from my neck into my shoulders and enjoying this warm feeling I drift into a deeper and deeper level of relaxation ...... the feeling of relaxation passes down through my shoulders to my arms reaching down to the tips of my fingers ...... my arms are now feeling tired and heavy as I sink into a deeper and deeper state of relaxation .... now my chest muscles are relaxed too and my stomach muscles ...... I focus on the gentle rise and fall of my stomach muscles as I slowly breath in and out .... now this warm relaxed feeling flows through my legs .... I notice how relaxed my limbs have become ...... my mind has become totally still and deeply, deeply relaxed ...... I concentrate on how my body feels while I enjoy this deep state of relaxation .... I am feeling lighter and lighter ...... floating higher and higher into a deeper level of relaxation ...... I am now completely relaxed .... more relaxed than I have ever felt before ...... as I experience this beautiful feeling of peace and calm ...... I will just let go of my mind ...... drift, relax and drift ....

Now that I am totally, deeply relaxed and at peace with myself ...... I will imagine myself in my special place ...... this is a very special place for me ...... it is very peaceful and calm and filled with tranquillity ...... being in my special place makes me very calm and relaxed ..... now I that I am completely at ease and relaxed .... I think about my fear of exams .... and all the worry and anxiety it's causing me .... the extreme nervousness .... exams are part of life and there is nothing to be afraid of ...... they are part of testing my knowledge and ability ...... for my good and benefit .... they are just tests .... providing me with an opportunity for me to practice and recall ...... with no harm at all ...... I imagine my exams coming up very soon and studying hard ...... getting prepared for them .... the more I practice and revise the less anxious I feel about them ...... I know I have given myself a big chance of passing them ...... because the art of passing an exam is knowing what your examiner wants ....and I will pass them .... the more I think about them the more relaxed and confident I get .... now my examination day arrives ..... I wake up feeling relaxed, calm and prepared for what's lying ahead ..... I know I will do well because I am well prepared .... I imagine myself walking into the examination room feeling very relaxed, calm and at peace with myself with no nerves at all .... I start my exam and I am focused and collected .... in fact I can remember everything that I revised ...... all the questions are clearly stated ...... I know a lot of answers to the questions and that gives me even more confidence as I go along .... I take one question at a time and I know that I will do well ...... I am able to remember all I have learned and recall the collect answers to the questions with ease because I am well prepared ...... the answers come to me easily and I remember all the information I need ...... and as I conclude my test I double check all my answers .... I am very satisfied that I have given all the right answers and I am very proud of myself .... and as I leave the examination room I feel a sense of pride and accomplishment flow through me ...... I am smiling because I have overcome my fear with determination ...... and from now on I will not be nervous and anxious when taking exams ...... anytime I feel nervous I will simply breath in and out and all the nervousness will fade away .... I know that I am strong and can overcome any challenges that come my way ...... I am free of my fear ....I will enjoy my special place for another moment ...... take all these positive feelings in ...... and bring them back with me ..... drift and float ...... I am feeling calm and relaxed ......

In a few minutes when I am ready to come back to full awareness ...... I will count from one to ten .... and as count from one to ten ...... will come back feeling totally relaxed ....

1 ....I am beginning to come back
2 .... The background noises are coming back
3 .... Feeling relaxed
4 .... I am aware of my body
5 .... Calm and peaceful
6 ....I am almost fully alert now

7 ....Feeling relaxed

8 ....I am aware of my normal surroundings

9 ....Beginning to open my eyes now

10 ....I open my eyes and come back feeling wonderful

FEAR OF EXAMINATIONS AFFIRMATIONS

- I am ready for my exams
- I am well prepared for whatever will come my way in the exams
- I believe I can do it
- I will pass my exams
- I am a person of great strength and determination
- Passing my exams will come easy for me
- I will turn my nerves into positive energy
- I am confident and intelligent
- I am more than capable of passing my exams
- I know what I need to know for the exams
- I am very focused in my preparations for my exams
- I will sail through my exams with ease
- My memory is perfect and I can recall will ease
- I will do well in my exams
- I am well prepared for my exams
- I feel good in myself and in control
- I plan my study schedule and will stick to it
- I believe in myself and will do my best
- I will succeed in my exams
- I will triumph in my exams
- My fear of exams is long gone
- I am a successful person
- I have achieved many goals in my life and I can easily achieve this as well
- I will be calm and relaxed in my exams
- I will be confident in my exams
- I will be in control of my emotions and nerves
- I am confident to pass my exams
- I will pass my exams

****

RESOURCES

https://hypnosis.edu/articles/healing.com/

www.hypnotherapy-directory.org.uk/articles/weightloss.html

www.nhs.uk/livewell/weight-loss-guide

www.nosmokingday.org-uk/health-benefits

www.nhs.uk/livewell/smoking

www.nhs.uk/conditions/Addictions

www.counselling-directory.org.uk/addictions.html

www.counselling-directory.org.uk/phobia.html

www.netdoctor.co.uk

www.mindorg.uk

www.deepscythe.com/2011/06/hypnosis-mental-health.html

www.who.int/tobacco/research/cessation/en/

American Journal of Epidemiology

················

Index

....